Praise for Lea ~~~~~~~~~~~~~~~~~~~~~~ ......un

"I believe that you have to love your people enough to preach the gospel to them—honestly, courageously, and, yes, prophetically right now to the very times in which we live. Will Willimon believes that, too, and says every pastor should lead by preaching. In these times, in particular, we need preachers who will preach the truth of Jesus Christ—all of it."

Jim Wallis, founder and editor-in-chief, *Sojourners*

"One of the great preachers of our time shows the intimate linkage between preaching and leadership, showing the synergies that emerge from seeing preaching as leadership. In an era when we desperately need our words to be appropriate to the Word, and to show the effects of those words in discipleship, Will Willimon charts an exciting and faithful path for preachers who lead, and leaders who preach!"

L. Gregory Jones, Dean and Williams
Distinguished Scholar, Duke Divinity School

"Will Willimon's argument connecting preaching and leadership is fundamental to ministry. Connecting preaching *and* leadership is as basic as connecting hearing and doing. The encounter with Christ is meant to change people and communities. 'The word preached leads to the word performed.' Worthy stuff in a church often unsure of its connection to God's presence and power."

Gil Rendle, author of *Quietly Courageous:*
Leading the Church in a Changing World

"Will Willimon is right: *to preach is to lead.* The arts of preaching and leading are interwoven with the sermon, well-crafted and well-delivered, taking its rightful place as the first task of the clergy leader. Preachers, read and be renewed in your calling to this wondrous work."

Hope Morgan Ward, bishop, North Carolina Conference, United Methodist Church

"*Leading with the Sermon* breaks new ground in exploring the ways that the practice of preaching and the exercise of adaptive leadership are intimately related. Willimon's passion for proclamation, his vivid storytelling, and his rich pastoral wisdom are evident on every page."

Angela Dienhart Hancock, Pittsburgh Theological Seminary

"William H. Willimon keeps his eye firmly on what is too often forgotten: leading a congregation—together with its call, task, and effectiveness—begins with the preaching of the Word of God. This book helpfully serves as an antidote to the widespread separation of pastoral preaching and leadership, as well as an immunization against the temptation to think of them more as personal accomplishments than gifts from God for the church."

Kimlyn J. Bender, George W. Truett Theological Seminary, Baylor University

LEADING
WITH THE
SERMON

LEADING
WITH THE
SERMON

Preaching as Leadership

WILLIAM H. WILLIMON

Fortress Press
Minneapolis

LEADING WITH THE SERMON
Peaching as Leadership

Print ISBN: 978-1-5064-5637-9
eBook ISBN: 978-1-5064-5638-6

All Scripture citations are from the Common English Bible, unless otherwise
noted.

Cover design: Emily Harris Designs
Typesetting: PerfecType, Nashville, TN

To my students in the
Introduction to Christian Leadership classes
of the Duke Doctor of Ministry Program

TABLE OF CONTENTS

PREFACE

One Monday morning Stanley Hauerwas ("America's best theologian," *Time*) asked, "Why don't you preachers utilize the sermon as an opportunity to lead?"

Stanley's question is the catalyst for this book.

While preaching is the most important job of pastors, preaching does more work than preaching. While proclamation must be biblical, true to the Christian faith's peculiar take on reality, a faithful sermon aspires to be more than a cool consideration of interesting spiritual ideas. Though the point of preaching is to speak about the God who has spoken to us in Jesus Christ, when we proclaim Jesus Christ, we also lead people who have been convened, converted, and commissioned by Christ.

My aim is to show how preaching aids and shapes our leadership and how our leadership provides the context, purposes, and test of our preaching. Sometimes I'll view leadership through the lens of preaching; elsewhere, I'll look at preaching as the practice of leadership in order to encourage working preachers.

While I'll draw upon the work of some of the best guides in both fields, I'll also rely upon my experience over four decades of pastoral leadership. As a seminary professor, I've been privileged to prepare hundreds of pastors. As a bishop overseeing six hundred preachers, I became convinced that while preaching is the most important work of pastors, leadership is one of our greatest inadequacies.

Preaching is a role to which none can aspire, a responsibility no one can choose. So is Christian leadership. My hope is to distill what I've learned about preaching and leading as a working preacher in order to instill fresh enthusiasm and confidence in my colleagues who, because God has called them to be pastors, must also be leaders, whether they want to or not.

Will Willimon

1

Preaching: The Most Important Leadership Activity of Pastors

"The chair of my church board said to me, 'I don't get a damn thing out of church.' Does that man's comment speak to any of you?" Thus my sermon's hastily concocted opening.

Before you judge me for my vulgar lead-in, hear the context. I was guest preacher at Pepperdine University's required chapel. My student congregation's posture, facial expressions, and open newspapers filled me with dread.

"I'm a dead man," said I to the Lord. "Please, Holy Spirit, give me something that will compel them to put down their newspapers. I'm begging." The sermon's first sentence was the only thing God gave me. After a collective gasp, their wandering adolescent eyes were fixed upon me and I was off to the races, laying a sermon upon them that they had assumed they didn't want.

Here's how God suggested I provocatively open this book: *Preaching is the most important task of an ordained leader.*

Preaching is at the center of pastoral work not only because in preaching a pastor is with more members of the congregation, in a more intentional and focused way, than in any other pastoral activity, making the pastor's unique role visibly, definitively evident. Proclamation is at the center because of who God is and what God is up to. We know the truth about God only because of the proclamation of the one true preacher, Jesus.

The pastor who pleads, "Though I'm not much of a preacher, I am a loving, caring pastor," is lying. There's no way to care for God's people as pastor without loving them enough to tell them the truth about God, what God is up to in the world, and how they can hitch on.

Christianity is a "revealed religion"; it happens when humanity is confronted by a loquacious God. We are unable to think about a Trinitarian God on our own. The truth about God must be revealed, spoken to us as the gift of a God who refuses to be vague or coy. It is of the nature of the Trinity to be communicative, revelatory—the Father speaking to the Son, the Son mutually interacting with the Father, all in the power of the Holy Spirit, God speaking to God's world.

A primary means of God's revelation is preaching.

The Christian life is characterized as address and response, so listening is one of the primary obligations of a practicing Christian. Our existence is subservient to and dependent upon the speech of a relentlessly self-revealing God. As Eugene Peterson frequently told us, with this God, square one is always "And God said . . ."[1]

The Self-Revealing God

We have preaching because of the God we've got. Whatever the Trinity wants from creatures or creation, God does it through words. Preaching is God talk, our talk about God and God's talk to us. We preach because God speaks, and God's self-selected way of speaking is through preaching. If preaching works, it's due to God. As Paul put it, "Because of this, neither the one who plants nor the one who waters is anything, but the only one who is anything is God who makes it grow" (1 Cor 3:7). We preachers never work alone, thank God. What's our major evidence that God is love? God speaks to us. What's a chief purpose of the church and its ministry? To provide an audience for God so that the whole church might be equipped to be preachers who speak up for God. God talks mainly through preaching.

> In the beginning was the Word
> and the Word was with God
> and the Word was God.
> The Word was with God in the beginning.
> Everything came into being through the Word,
> and without the Word
> nothing came into being.
> What came into being
> through the Word was life,
> and the life was the light for all people. (John 1:1–4)

In this majestic opening of John's Gospel we hear an echo of the sermon that opens Genesis 1:1–3: "When God began to create the heavens and the earth—the earth was without shape or form, it was dark over the deep sea, and God's wind swept over the waters—God said, 'Let there be light.'"

There are gods who create worlds by having sex with other gods, or through a primal, cosmic battle between good and evil, chaos and order. The Trinity creates through sovereign, efficacious, nonviolent words. God just says "Light!" and there is something out of nothing, due to words. That the world *is* rather than *isn't* is testimony to God's loquaciousness. Preaching, the Genesis of everything.

On a cloudless night God called Abram out of his tent and preached a promise to make a great nation from this childless old man and his aged wife Sarai, a people out of no people (Gen 15:1–6). Words are the way God works.

Later, with Abram's progeny under the heel of the most powerful empire in the world, God comes to Moses out in Midian (Exod 3:1–11). Before dumbfounded Moses, a bush bursts into flame, but the bush is unconsumed. Even more astounding, the bush talks: "I am the Lord your God. I have heard the cry of my people and have come down to liberate them. Now, you go to the pharaoh and tell him to let my people go."

That's all? God frees the Hebrews on the basis of nothing but a speech from a none-too-talented, untrained preacher, the murderer Moses? Moses justifiably wants to know, "Who am I that I should go to the pharaoh and say . . . ?"

This is how this God works, creating something out of nothing, a people out of nobodies, free women and men out of slaves with mere words uttered by conscripted preachers.

The now free Hebrews are given a land "full of milk and honey," just as God had sovereignly promised. But they wandered. They consorted with other gods, forgot their origins, disdained the God who had blessed them. So, God sent a peculiar band of preachers called "prophets"—God-obsessed individuals enlisted by God to give Israel the bad news of coming exile, then to sustain them through the horrors of Babylonian captivity, only to announce the gospel of home-coming, then to direct how they would reconstruct themselves as God's people—all on the basis of nothing but words. The prophets of Israel were poets, preachers deconstructing old worlds and envisioning new worlds with some of the pushi-est and the most poetic, figurative, and powerful speech ever uttered. Just words.

The word of the Lord not only creates but also devastates. Jeremiah is called *in utero* to be "a prophet to the nations." Jer-emiah protests, "I don't know how to speak." The Lord encour-ages (threatens?) Jeremiah by reminding the nascent prophet that preaching originates with God, not us:

> "Don't say, 'I'm only a child.'
> Where I send you, you must go;
> what I tell you, you must say.
> Don't be afraid of them, . . . I'm putting my words in
>   your mouth."

Then the Lord makes Jeremiah not only a preacher but a world leader:

> "This very day I appoint you over nations and empires,
> to dig up and pull down,
> to destroy and demolish,
> to build and plant." (Jer 1:5–10)

Empires demolished or established with nothing but God's word in human words? What a high view of human speech com-mandeered by God.

In the Bible, word precedes world. There is nothing until there is creative speech. Reality is linguistically constructed. Words do not arise from things; things are evoked by the word. God said, "Let there be light." And there was. Yahweh allowed the earthling, Adam, to enjoy a bit of divine creativity by naming the cattle and birds (Gen 2:20). Creativity is a word-derived phenomenon. Anything God wants done among us begins with "And God said . . ."

God's Work through Words

There came One among us, Emmanuel, God with us, Word Made Flesh. Jesus's work? He came preaching (Matt 4:17). His first assault upon the world-as-it-is was in a pulpit, quoting his favorite prophet: "The Spirit of the Lord is upon me . . . to preach good news" (Luke 4:18). Whatever good God means to do, God does most of it through Spirit-induced words.

Jesus assaulted the world, not with violent deeds but by a barrage of words—parables that shocked, evoked, amused, and disclosed; sermons that sometimes ended with a riot; warnings, blessings, curses, proverbs, and prophecies so true that they made the congregation want to kill the preacher. He said he brought a new kingdom, and some—not many of the wise and powerful, but enough to attract the jittery attention of the bigwigs—hailed him as "King." All he did to inaugurate his reign was to speak nonviolently.

His metaphors were sometimes obscure, his parables hard to follow, and his meaning elusive, but he spoke clearly enough for the governmental and religious authorities to get his point. They crucified him in an attempt to shut him up.

For three days the silence was deafening.

The accounts of what happened on the third day after his crucifixion are diverse and confusing, as if the witnesses do not know how to say what they had seen and heard. Some women (where were the men?) came to his tomb in the early morning darkness and in grief to pay their respects to the body of poor, beaten, dead Jesus. There, they were met by an impudent angel who smirked, "Why do you seek the living among the dead?"

The heavenly messenger did not say, "He is risen! Now you will get to see your loved ones when you die." The Easter message was a homiletical commission: "Go, tell . . ." (Mark 16:7).

The Christian practice of proclamation was born in the resurrection. His disciples thought the cross was the end of the conversation; by God's grace, it was a new beginning. Time and again in our history with God, when we betrayed the love of God—with our infidelity or misunderstanding, or when the world intimidated us into silence, when we have fled into the darkness or stopped up our ears and hardened our hearts—this talkative God returned to us and resumed the conversation. Thus incarcerated Paul prayed not that God would get him out of jail but that God might "open a door for the word so we can preach" (Col 4:3). Paul knew that preaching—divine-human—conversation, is always at God's initiative, not ours.

In that dialogue between heaven and earth, God has proved remarkably resourceful and imaginative, master of stratagems and devices—the Incarnation, Word Made Flesh, being the most ingenious of all. God refuses to be trapped in heaven or confined to monologue. There is a relentlessness about the speech of this God, an effusive loquaciousness, a dogged determination not to fall silent, nor to cease preaching, until the whole world joins in.

Therein is our hope: the verbal business between us and God is restarted and sustained at every turn by a living, resourceful, long-winded God, thank God.

The church, despite its sins of silence, has never been able to stifle God's revelation. In every age, including our own—even amid the desolation of mainline Protestant church decline, even when having to work with the poorest of preachers—God has found a way to talk to God's church. Church talk to and about God ensures that people know the truth about God, that God has a people, and that God's will be done on earth as in heaven. If God should stop talking, if God should withdraw into apophatic, sullen silence, death would have the final say. Yet God's creative, life-giving, people-forming, intrusive word continues creating, keeps being made flesh, pushes in, and has the last word. "Go, tell!"

Preacher Isaiah hears a divine promise: "My word that comes from my mouth . . . does not return to me empty. Instead, it does what I want, and accomplishes what I intend" (Isa 55:11). A promise or a threat? Preacher, make the call.

When Paul's leadership was challenged by some in Galatia, Paul's defense was his commission as spokesperson for God: "I want you to know that the gospel I preached isn't human in origin. I didn't receive it or learn it from a human. It came through a revelation from Jesus Christ" (Gal 1:11–12).

Paul defends himself as an apostle, but Paul's apology applies to every apostolic leader and preacher of the gospel. Our ultimate authorization rests not upon an orthodox, faithful reiteration of church tradition; not by seminary certification; not upon official confirmation by ecclesiastical execs. We lead "through a revelation from Jesus Christ." So brash, audacious a claim for one's speech could tempt the claimant to self-delusion. In every age the church has rightly asked its leaders, "How do we know your words are from God rather than from yourself?" Yet, upon this scandalous, ambiguously incarnational affirmation rests the function of preaching and the basis for the authority of the Christian leader. A Savior who is fully human and completely divine provokes such paradoxes.

As Bullinger asserts in the Second Helvetic Confession: "The preaching of the word of God *is* the Word of God." This is an astounding claim for the speech of mere mortals like preachers and for the hearing of self-deceitful listeners like our congregations. Yet it is no more astonishing than Jesus's promise to the apostles: "Whoever listens to you listens to me" (Luke 10:16). Paul's boast that "we do not proclaim ourselves" (2 Cor 4:5 NRSV) arises not from self-confidence but rather from faith in a gracious God who condescends to mere mortals through preaching, from trust in the truth of a story that begins with "And God said . . ."

Sermons That Summon

Though preaching's inception is theological—God's word to humans—preaching's means are anthropological—human words about God. It is not enough to hear or even to agree to God's word; God's word is always an address whereby we are summoned, enlisted, called by God to be other than who we were born to be. Preachers therefore aim not just for our listeners' assent but for human embodiment, performance, and practice of the assertions of the sermon. What Christopher Beeley says for a leader applies to preachers as well: "The spiritual condition of the flock is the only real measure of a leader's success"[2]—a canon of measurement that sends a chill down my spine as I assess my own congregation.

Still, my sermons are to be judged by the quality of the disciples my preaching produces.

Jesus's command was "Follow me!" Reception of the divine gospel demands human enactment of the gospel, discipleship. Salvation is vocation. Jesus means more than "God is love"; Jesus is God's love in action, God's love as vocation. His message was a summons: "Come, join up, take part in God's reclamation of God's creation." Whatever Jesus wants done in the world, Jesus elects not to do it alone. The vocative, missional intent of preaching (derived from the nature of the gospel itself) is why, from the first days of Jesus's earthly ministry, *preaching and leadership are inseparable.*

In preaching, God's people are moved, that is, *led*—little by little, or sometimes violently jolted—in the power of the Holy Spirit, Sunday by Sunday, toward new and otherwise unavailable descriptions of reality. Every sermon potentially offers a new heaven and a new earth. The complaint "Your sermon didn't really speak to my world" overlooks the potentially disruptive, dislocating power of preaching that wants to rock our world.

A pragmatic, typically American charge against Christian preaching is that Christians fail to "practice what they preach." Fair criticism, as long as the critic understands that Christians are always amateurs, always on our way, tagging along behind the God who, though always going on ahead of us, leading us (Mark 10:32), refuses to leave us be.

Sermons are summons repeatedly addressed to God's people on the way. Christian preaching is not merely the skillful description of the world as it is, but a bold, visionary, and demanding call to move toward a world that is to be. The result of proclamation is performance of the faith, and we are not—in most of our performances—there yet. Christian preachers are heralds who proclaim the true sovereignty of God in territory whose ownership is under dispute. Jesus Christ is Lord, but not in fullness and completion. It's easy to point to the gap between what Christians profess ("Jesus Christ is Lord") and how we presently live ("The United States is synonymous with the kingdom of God"). There's always a gap, a contested space, between our designation as "the body of Christ" and the empirical reality of the poor old church.

Do not accuse us of hypocrisy when we say more than we are able to live. Our discipleship is aspirational, provisional, constantly under threat. Of course we say more than we are in the faith, that by the grace of God, one day we shall be more than we could have been without the repeated summons to "follow me!" In any age, the church never outgrows its first name, "the Way" (Acts 9:2).

From our earliest days, it was not enough for preachers to articulate the good news of Jesus Christ; they also had to step up, accept responsibility, and take the initiative to be forerunners in embodiment of the gospel they were preaching. Somebody had to answer the call to lead because the gospel requires more than admiring bystanders or passersby (the religious leaders of the parable of the Good Samaritan). Like the Samaritan who refused to pass by and who risked taking responsibility for someone he didn't even know, Christian leaders attend to, bind up the wounds of, and make the sacrifices required to empower others not only to accept but also to embody the gospel.

Because preacher Jesus preached, "You are the salt of the earth. . . . You are the light of the world. . . . Let your light shine before people, so they can see the good things you do and praise your Father who is in heaven" (Matt 5:13–16), leadership is required.

Because Paul preached the radical, "God was reconciling the world to himself through Christ" (2 Cor 5:19), calling us "to the ministry of reconciliation" (5:18), Paul had to roll up his sleeves and learn how to be a church planter.

It's not good enough to clearly communicate important religious ideas; not enough for the sermon to ask and answer, "Who is God and what is God up to in the world?" The sermon must also be invitational: "Don't you want to hitch on to what God is doing?" At some point in sermons, God's people must hear the summons "Let's go!"

Preaching as Confrontation

When Paul the missionary leader/preacher opens his address to the Corinthians with "I thank my God always for you" (1 Cor 1:4), that doesn't stop Paul from enumerating all the ways the Corinthians fall short in their embodiment of the gospel. Paul refuses either to trim his proclamation to the Corinthians' meager abilities to live what they profess or to let any of the Corinthians' virtues deter him from wanting more. Paul was better than an articulator of interesting ideas about Jesus; Paul was a missionary leader. Paul's letters, sermons, and theological concepts were in service to the creation and sustenance of a living, breathing, active body of Christ.

It's not enough for a preacher to urge people to have more open and accepting attitudes toward LGBTQ+ persons. The pastor must do the mundane work required to create a real community where all persons are not only welcomed but also joined to and empowered to play their part in Jesus's work in the world. The one who preaches must become the one who leads.

The Roman Empire did not persecute the first Christians for believing screwball spiritual ideas. Caesar tried to stamp out Christ's followers because Christian leaders encouraged "unlearned and ignorant" rabble (Acts 4:13 KJV) to step out, act up, join up, and move out in ways that were troublingly antipatriotic.

P. T. Forsyth thunders forth in his 1907 Beecher Lectures that through the preacher Christ preaches so that the church can preach:

> The one great preacher in history, I would contend, is the Church. And the first business of the individual preacher is to enable the Church to preach that the Church may become a missionary to the world.[3]

The violent reaction of the congregation to Jesus's first sermon (Luke 4) is a reminder that preaching in the name of Jesus Christ usually spells trouble. A faithful sermon is what God wants to say, in the power of the Holy Spirit, rather than what we want to hear. Just as there is no transformative leadership without conflict, there is no conversion without friction. The gospel is, as Luther said, the *verbum externum*, an external word, a word that is not innate, not common sense, a word that we cannot speak to ourselves.

The Good News is good news/bad news depending upon the hearer's context. For everyone who hears the words of Jesus gladly, repents, and comes forth to walk the way of Christ, many more sneer, "Where did this man get all this?" (Matt 13:56). The quest for the absolutely effective, universally well-received sermon is as delusional as the desire to be the universally beloved Christian leader, not because nobody can please everybody but because there's no such thing as a less-than-crucified Messiah.

As Bonhoeffer said, there is only one preacher: Christ. Because preaching is proclamation of the word of God, it is more than moral exhortation (the gospel reduced to prescriptions for human behavior), more than heartfelt expression of the preacher's personal struggles (who cares?). Preaching requires creativity beyond skillful explanation and representation of God's word (the task of theology). Preaching is not, despite the history of rhetoric, primarily a matter of persuasive speaking; persuasive speaking and positive listener response are God's problem, not ours.

Preaching allows the risen Christ to walk among his people and to have his way with their lives.

Whether God speaks through preaching is God's free, sovereign choice.

A sower goes forth to sow and, without careful preparation or planning, begins slinging seed (Matt 13:1–9). Of course, in such effusive sowing, there is much waste. The sower risks failure. Most of the seed falls on infertile ground in the sower's intent to overwhelm the world with words. It is up to God to give growth, not us preachers. The hearing of God's word is not an example of democracy in action, with the hearers making savvy choices about what they will accept or reject. Preaching is dramatic, effusive, reckless presentation of God's word, so that God's word might be heard through it, if God wills.

It's annoying when the congregation is unable or refuses to hear. Some of their incomprehension of the gospel is due to Jesus (surely our preaching task would be easier if God had not come to us as a Jew from Nazareth who lived briefly, died violently, and rose unexpectedly). Some of our listeners' befuddlement is due to their hardness of heart and to their being so well defended against the truth who is Jesus Christ. Relatively affluent, upper-middle-class North America is a tough neighborhood. Look at our statistics.

Still, my congregation is no worse than the primordial "formless void" (Gen 1:2 NRSV), or the unsavory cast of characters to whom Christ returned in his resurrection—that is, the very ones who disappointed and betrayed him throughout his ministry. If my congregational composition is limited to the not-too-oppressed and not-too-needy, I should be unsurprised when the gospel falls upon deaf ears. If, on the other hand, my leadership in evangelism and witness has been so effective that I throw my voice out to an assemblage of the wretched of the earth, the lame and the blind, the sorrowful and the marginalized, fools and the walking dead, then I am blessed with just the sort of folk Jesus enjoys surprising with "Follow me."

A Mutual Endeavor

Like preaching, leadership is a shared undertaking. Preachers are in a reciprocal relationship with their listeners. Leaders not only influence their constituency but also bend under its influence. Most congregations have many ways—cute comments, well-meaning but cutting asides, sinister glances—of attempting to tame the preacher. That we preachers receive a hearing from the congregation is, in great part, a gift of the congregation. That preachers dare to speak up and speak out, in spite of congregational censure or resistance, is a credit to the work of the Holy Spirit.

Leaders are servants who allow the organization's needs to take precedence over their own, who learn and then dare to provide the most appropriate leadership for the organization at this time and place. Particularly in the church, where the pastor often leads by convening and empowering lay congregational leaders, leadership occurs in concert with others rather than as self-expression of the heroic traits of the lone leader. Most of pastoral authority is bestowed, granted, or offered; all preaching is dialogical.

Throughout the history of the church's preaching, one senses a certain nervousness within the church, a recurring lament over the state of preaching. The church is right to worry about its preaching because every Sunday sermon is an experiment, a public test of the church's claim that Jesus Christ was indeed raised from the dead and continues to call the very ones who betray him. Either my preaching produces one credible Christian every decade or so or mine is a life wasted.

If embodiment, performance, of the gospel is the test of preaching's fidelity, then my proclamation of God's word is ground zero for the detonation called church. I can do many things well in my leadership, but if God refuses to construct the church through my preaching, I receive no greater accolade than being dubbed an effective manager of an efficient volunteer organization.

Preaching sets the terms under which my congregation can justly be called a church. In each Sunday's sermon the church is reminded of who it is and to whom it is accountable. Preaching reiterates the identity and the mission of the church and enables Christians to discern and differentiate the story that forms and ever reforms the church as God's.

In Mark 3:14–15, Jesus calls the disciples: "He appointed twelve and called them apostles. He appointed them to be with him, to be sent out to preach, and to have authority to throw out demons." Three cardinal purposes of the church are in evidence: we are convened; Jesus speaks to us, commissioning us; and then we are sent, scattered as Christ's witnesses. By his word, we are gathered and told who we are; at his word we are commissioned, sent out to speak his word. The preacher preaches to the church on Sunday so that the laity might proclaim Christ to the world all week.

With the gradual establishment of western Christendom, gathering became the primary dynamic of the church with a loss of the essential linkage between the gathered church and the scattered church. Congregations lost a sense of sent-ness, with a concomitant loss of missional vocation. Churches languished by turning inward and allowing their primary responsibility to be to their members rather than to the world for whom Christ died. Rather than being salt and light, we became honey to help the world's solutions go down easier. Who needs preaching for that? Leadership is not needed to guide people in a direction they are already headed.

I know of no church that goes forth from the cozy confines of their contented congregation toward a world dying for want of the gospel without someone who is willing not only to preach but also to lead.

It may be possible for Christians to be convened, identified, instructed, and commissioned in ways other than through preaching, though it's not probable. As Paul asked, "How can they hear without a preacher?" (Rom 10:14). Somebody must step up and take responsibility for leading through preaching. It's not Christian preaching if the preacher is not also willing to move from proclaiming the gospel to leading the performance of the gospel.

And guess whom God has chosen both to lead and to preach?

2

Preachers Are Leaders

"What are the issues that the church must confront?" I ask seminarians.

"Sexism." "Racism." "Poverty," they call out.

I pause for effect, then assert histrionically, "*None* of that will change without someone taking responsibility, stepping up, and leading."

Leadership is the art of using words to influence, organize, orchestrate, and motivate people to face their problems. The pastor who pleads, "I'm a preacher of God's word; I don't bother with administrative, management stuff" shows an inadequate theology of the word. There's no way to preach God's word without also leading the congregation in embodying the word, provoking movement from truth-hearing to truth-enacting in an actual congregation. Disembodied, unperformed speech is cheap.

Leadership is necessary only if a group is under orders to go somewhere. Without a mission, there is no need for leaders. The skill of leadership required by an organization is in proportion to the danger and difficulty of the organization's mission. It's easier to enlist an adequate leader for the Men's Garden Club than for a US Army platoon, less risky to be president of General Motors than pastor of St. John's on the Expressway.

The main motivation for preachers' acquisition of leadership skills is the vocation of Jesus Christ. Thus care must be exercised in correlating church leadership with that of any other institution; the church is an alien colony with few allies among the world's ways of gathering and empowering people. Only cautiously can the church's ordained leaders take their cues from secular models of leadership because our leading is under orders to be congruent with and accountable to the leadership of Christ.

And yet, because we are under Christ's mandate to be faithful by being fruitful, Christian leaders are not free to dismiss out of hand any insight or skill that will enable the church to be more fruitful. Ecclesial inefficiency not only wastes time and money but is also an offense against the urgency of Christ's rapidly encroaching kingdom. Inept leadership hinders our obedience to Christ's "Go and make disciples of all nations . . ." (Matt 28:19). Damage is done to well-meaning disciples by ill-equipped leaders. Poorly run meetings, lax financial oversight, absence of accountability, sorry supervision of staff, and poor time management are frequent complaints from laity about pastors. "Remember, the church is not a business. Leadership techniques that work in the world don't work in the vineyard of the Lord" is often a cover for a stubborn unwillingness to serve God's people by learning to lead.

In leading God's people, preachers move from *didache*, *kerygma*, and *doxa* to praxis. As challenging as good preaching is, competent, skilled, courageous leadership can be even more daunting for pastors. It's tough to craft an interesting sermon;

equally demanding to lead a productive church meeting. All Christian leadership's authority is contested because it rests upon Christ's still-disputed sovereignty. No matter how skilled their leadership, Christian leaders can expect trouble because it's leadership in the name of Jesus, the world's troublemaker.

Leading by Talking

It's all too easy for preachers to evade responsibility for gaining the skills and insights required to lead in embodiment and instigation of the congregation. Our ministerial training presented theology as abstract, disembodied ideas and spirituality as a set of personal practices. Most of us received our theological education from seminary professors who had little or no leadership and management experience, which may account for why many theological professors demean the acquisition of practical leadership skills.

Pastors can't be theologians without being leaders. Jesus won't allow his people to be victims of a disembodied word, a static, stay-at-home God, or enslavement to the status quo as a substitute for the adventure of playing our part in Christ's new creation. Paul didn't just write letters; he built up congregations. An early Christian preacher like Mark or Luke didn't write merely to convey religious ideas: "Don't you agree?" Their Gospels were vocational: "Join up!" followed by, "Let's go!"

Against all docetic, disincarnate tendencies, the church has always affirmed that Christ is fully, completely human, embodied, without diminution of his divinity. We must resist the docetic temptation to disdain concern with administrative, managerial leadership of the church—Jesus Christ is really, fully, completely human; disembodied faith is not faith in him.

But being Chalcedonian Christians, we also must affirm that the mission of the church is utterly impossible without a Jesus who is really, fully, completely divine. His body, though crucified, is where the Holy Spirit descended in bodily form (Luke 3:22) and in whom the fullness of God chooses to dwell (Col 2:9). There is no God hiding behind the Incarnation, holding anything back from humanity. Jesus actually is God coming for us, God in motion, more God than we can handle, God refusing to be vague or insubstantial, God with a body, God so near as to demand human response. A merely human Jesus reduces Christian leadership to what solely human efforts can achieve. Any weakening of the divine in Christ results in indecision and uncertainty, a fatal, equivocal, indistinct vagueness that is the death of leadership in Jesus's name.

Just as some wish Jesus had not come as a Jew, had not refused self-defense and violence, had not turned his back on wealth and worldly power, had not said so many unkind things about religious leaders like me, many wish Jesus had not made the poor old church his bride and body—his great plan for what's wrong with the world. We can't dismiss Jesus's teachings with, "Well, he was God, so forgiveness of enemies was easy for him." Jesus was fully, completely human. He calls us to follow him in this world, now, rather than passively wait for him to give us the next.

Jesus is also fully God. Many of our churches languish because they've tried to cut God down to our size, reducing the Trinity to a rather trivial, allegedly concerned, but essentially inactive God. They attempt to achieve only that which is humanly feasible. They venture nothing so bold and brash that they risk utter, embarrassing failure *unless* the Easter women evangelists were right and Jesus Christ has bodily risen from the dead. Hesitant, circumspect ecclesiology leads to a limp and trifling Christology.

A flaccid Christology produces just another human institution, and preachers become no more than unctuous members of the helping professions.

What God expects the church to do among suffering humanity can't be done by humanity alone. The church is a human institution but not merely that. The kingdom of God cannot be devised by human efforts, even by very skilled leadership. Any God who is less than the one who raised Jesus from the dead is no match for the deadly, demonic resistance to the reign of God. What God means to do among us is more, so much more, than the production of even a well-functioning organization. I tell you, if God were not in Christ, reconciling the world, then attempting to preach to or to lead a church is the dumbest of undertakings.

Preachers are leaders because of the God we've got in Jesus Christ, the nature of God's realm, and the content of the gospel. Salvation in Jesus's name necessitates someone accepting Christ's yoke of leadership. The rationale for Christian leadership is theological. Anytime the church dares ask itself, "What doth the Lord require?" leadership is needed for the next step.

Still, in spite of the difficulties and dangers of leadership in the name of Jesus, it's wonderful to behold the word of God faithfully spoken, the Holy Spirit ripping the sermon out of our hands, and we get a front-row seat to watch the body of Christ set in motion.

> "You need to thank Preacher Baker for what he's done for you here," said Trinity's lay leader, the indomitable Peggy Hursey, as she welcomed me as pastor.
>
> "How would you characterize George Baker's leadership?" I asked Peggy.

"George told six or seven people to go to hell who no preacher had been man enough to tell where to get off. Now this church is ready to rock and roll," she replied.

As he gathered his books, George had advised, "Always do scales on the piano first thing on Sundays before you preach. Helps develop vocal range. With your scratchy voice, you need that. Keep your tempo up in a sermon; energy is contagious from the pulpit to the congregation. God knows this crowd needs energizing. One more thing, son: this crowd loves to fight. Bunch of Philistines. Keep 'em fighting the Devil or they'll turn and kill you!"

"How do I do that?" I asked in a trembling voice.

"Find out where Satan is in this town, tell 'em about it, and then turn 'em loose."

In less than two months, after a group of United Methodist women observed police brutality at the local jail, with help from Micah, I preached a sermon about the evils of corrupt law enforcement, citing our Lord as a noteworthy victim. I told 'em about it. Fighting back tears I said, "Two of our saints, Eleanor and Mary, this week engaging in their ministry at the jail, observed a policeman roughing up a young man in a back cell. When they complained to the chief, he actually said to these two saintly women that . . ." (eyes filled with tears, hardly able to speak) "'You church ladies look after your church stuff and I'll look after the jail.'"

Congregational gasp. Someone on the third pew shouts, "Busby's got two boats and an Eldorado on a cop's salary?"

"And a riding lawnmower!" added another.

I fully expected them to begin furiously tossing *Methodist Hymnals.*

"Now I can't speak for you," I continued, barely regaining my composure, "but I for one find it hard to sit back and let our dear church, and these dear women, be insulted by a questionable cop."

During the pandemonium I gave an altar call for anyone Jesus had summoned to aid him against cops gone bad and turned 'em loose. Body of Christ set in motion with nothing but words.[1]

If Jesus were not the foundation, cornerstone, convener, and head of the church, the church need not trouble itself about good leadership. The identity, purpose, and mission given by Christ to the church necessitate leadership more skilled and courageous than that required for other well-meaning nonprofit organizations. Jesus Christ keeps Christian leadership difficult.

Melville famously portrayed the pulpit as the prow of a great ship that leads the church into uncharted waters:

> The pulpit is ever this earth's foremost part; all the rest comes in its rear; the pulpit leads the world. From thence it is that the storm of God's quick wrath is first descried, and the bow must bear the earliest brunt. From thence it is that the God of breezes fair or foul is first invoked for favorable winds. Yes, the world's a ship on its passage out, and not a voyage complete; and the pulpit is its prow.[2]

South Carolina pastor Michael Turner preached the Sunday after the massacre at Mother Emanuel Church in Charleston, delving into uncharted waters. He chose to make his sermon an anguished confession, narrating the racist environment in which he had grown up and confessing his own struggle with inbred ideas of white superiority. Through painful confrontations with his own racial bias, Turner told the congregation that he realized, "I'm not exempt from racism. And neither are you. Now, I desperately don't want to be racist. I'm confident you don't want to be either, but we have been shaped and formed in racial ways of thinking."

After speaking further about the depths, the subtlety, and the power of white racism, Turner said, "But here's the good news. We don't have to be overcome by evil. We can overcome evil with good."[3] The pulpit as the prow.

When I visited a church, a dear person welcomed me with: "You will find us to be one of the friendliest, most warm and caring churches. We're like a family. When one of us is in need, people are there for them."

That's not good enough, I thought to myself. In my experience, the boast of being a warm, friendly, caring congregation often covers a lack of leadership required to be a fully functioning part of the mission of Christ.

Courage

After Jesus's baptism, he is forty days in the wilderness and resists the temptations of Satan (who had his own interesting definitions of leadership, Luke 4:1–13). Then Jesus inaugurates his ministry. How? By preaching the word (Luke 4:14–30) and calling a handful of ordinary, unskilled, woefully inept people like the fisherman Simon (later called Peter) to do the tasks he wants done: "Do not be afraid; from now on you will be fishing for people" (Luke 5:10).

Why did Jesus tell them not to fear? Jesus says, "I am going to take back the world, turn everything upside down in dramatic revolution, and reclaim the kingdom of God. And guess who is going to help me?" He then commands them not to be fearful; it takes guts to work with Jesus.

Fear of public speaking always makes the top of the list of phobias. Preachers get the shakes not out of fear of our audience, but due to Jesus. The message he commissions us to deliver is not for the faint of heart. Intestinal fortitude is required to preach provocative Jesus.

Thus Luther urged preachers of his day to "not be silent or mumble but testify without being frightened or bashful . . . speak out candidly without regarding or sparing anyone, let it strike whomever or whatever it will. It is a great hindrance to a preacher . . . [to] look around and worry about what people like or do not like to hear. . . ."[4] Gospel preaching on Sunday requires finding a way to talk about matters the congregation has excluded from conversation all week.

When I left seminary teaching, the bishop stuck me at Northside United Methodist Church, bragging to his buddies, "That will knock him down a notch or two. He won't be able to talk his way out of this."

"Poor Northside has set the record for attrition," said the sympathetic district superintendent. "Good luck."

Barely four hundred Methodists knocked around in a building built for two thousand. Most disheartening were the seven—count 'em, seven—empty Sunday school rooms, three of which were now used for storage, as if upon Jesus's return his first command would be "Quick. Bring me dozens of worn-out hymnals and all the rusting metal folding chairs you can carry. Come on, people, let's inaugurate the Reign of God!"

This is not only the sort of church dumped upon a pastor when one is ordained in mainline Protestantism but also when serving a Savior who is a sucker for—and a redeemer of—lost causes. Conversion, transformation, and renovation are what redemptive Jesus does to people and to their churches. A dying or dead church like Northside is just one more opportunity to witness the costly miracles worked by Mr. Resurrection and the Life (John 11:25).

After a year of assessment, I called a meeting of the church leadership. I showed them a decade of dismal statistics, all heading downward except for an upwardly soaring median age. According to my estimates, the last Methodist would turn out the lights on Northside sometime around 2020. There were tears, some anger (Methodists are typically unfailingly nice and repressed), and palpable anguish.

After allowing time for the facts to sink in, I said, "But the good news is I've got some workable, realistic ways we can help God give us a future. The bad news: none of the solutions is painless."

"Tell us more," someone said with a trembling voice.

I urged that we do away with all church offices and committees and slim down our governance to an eight-person task force. I would recommend who ought to be on the task force: those who knew how to start things, who didn't mind taking risks, and who could move with urgency.

I told them that our number one priority ought to be growth in membership. None of our problems—financial, morale, building maintenance, dearth of youth and children—could be solved without fixing our shrinking membership. Every dime we spent, the way I as a pastor apportioned my time, the test for every new initiative for the coming year was to be ruthlessly evaluated by one priority—growth.

That night we junked plans to refurbish the church parlor and, instead, put the funds into renovating the nursery and children's church school. I told them I would share the changes in how I spent my time in order to lead their priorities. I would work differently in order to lead what most needed to happen in the church.

I went on a crash church-growth reading course. I preached a sermon series, "Mission Possible," in which, just following the Common Lectionary, I noted the nature of Jesus as the embodiment of God's mission. Each sermon was heavy on examples of individuals and churches who got geared up for mission and evangelism. At the end of each sermon I said, "Okay. You've watched Jesus in action in mission. Now I want everyone, everyone, to take one of those cards in the pew rack and complete this sentence: *Because Jesus's mission was to _____, therefore Northside Church's mission should be to _____.* Drop your cards in the box at the back as you leave this service."

After a month of sermons, I changed the post-sermon response card to this sentence: *Because of the mission that Jesus has given to Northside Church, I will _____.*

We hired an evangelism consultant, who urged us to transform our children's ministry and to initiate a young adults group. Thirty new members were received in the first six months, and for the first time in the congregation's history, praise God, we pledged the budget in full. (During my stewardship sermon, I told them how much Patsy and I were pledging for the coming year—anything to shame them to up their giving.)

In service to the needs of Northside Church, I was forced to acquire skills I did not have, to reform my ministry, and to learn to be the leader I had not previously known how to be.

Recently I spent an hour with a young woman who, in her first six months as pastor of a small-town church, discovered that the congregation was in greater difficulty financially and demographically than they knew.

"How do I tell them the truth they've been denying without their hating me for it?" she asked. We discussed issues of timing, presentation, and strategies—topics remarkably similar to what goes through a preacher's head on the way to a sermon on a tough text. I was impressed with this pastor's determination to find a way to speak the life-giving truth that previous pastors had avoided.

"I give thanks to God that I'm not only a pastor but also a mother," she said. "Motherhood has given me lots of experience in telling painful truth to people I love."

Toward the end of our conversation I said, "Just a couple of decades ago, two preachers like us would not have had this conversation. The church has handed us some hard work that few of us expected and for which fewer of us are trained."

We may be the first generation of pastors in centuries to whom God has given the intimidating assignment not only to love but also to change the church. When the San Damiano crucifix spoke to Francis of Assisi, it didn't say, "Love everybody, particularly the birds." Christ ordered Francis, *Rebuild my church.*

That's us. Criticize us pastors for seizing uncritically upon secular leadership and management books, but at least give us credit for knowing that we have daunting, transformative work before us, tasks made more formidable because of who pastors are as persons and because of our inadequate training in leadership.

Preachers Are a Pain

A person emerged from our church a few Sundays ago, saying to me at the door as she left, "I know that you would not intentionally hurt anyone with what you say from the pulpit, but I was hurt by what you said in your sermon."

And I thought, "Where would you have gotten the notion that I don't want to hurt you? I'm a preacher. Infliction of pain comes with the job!" Luther compared the word of God to a surgeon's scalpel.[5]

Luke 4:16–30 stands as constant warning to us preachers and to our congregations. Preaching has to do, not simply with *our* words, but with the word of God, a scalpel that severs our settled arrangements, a word not of our own concoction. To be the recipient of that word is sometimes to be in pain because of it. As Luther said, here is a word that first kills in order to make alive, that damns in order to bless. Preaching is akin to surgery.

In high school I worked in a failing sporting goods store. My youthful brush with business convinced me that I was unsuited for commercial life. Bosses must hire and fire people, cut costs, reprimand unproductive employees, and have uncomfortable conversations. I was too nice for that.

Callow youth, I had the misapprehension that it was possible to be a pastor without having to hurt anybody—only one of my dumb beliefs at sixteen.

Leadership is necessary only if an organization needs to go somewhere and if an organization is accountable to a mission more important than its own survival. Many people in leadership positions vainly try to foster warm relationships or strive to be efficient managers rather than risk-taking leaders, not because they are so nice but rather because institutions crave the placidity of the status quo and reward those who keep them comfortable. Amicable caregiving (the default mode of most of us pastors) is less costly than courageous leading.

Trouble is, no human gathering survives or thrives without continual transformation, refitting, and repositioning—particularly an institution that's accountable to a living God.

Pastors have got to get over the fantasy that effective leadership is either innate—you're a natural-born leader or you're not—or a complex, insoluble mystery. The best practices and skills of congregational leadership can be learned. To the pastor who shuns responsibility by saying, "I have few talents for leadership, so I won't worry about that," the church says, "Did you think Jesus summons people to service on the basis of their talents? Leadership is only one of the skills you'll have to cultivate in obedience to your vocation."

A leader puts an organization in pain that it has been avoiding—utilizing its very best resources of avoidance—in the faith that the organization can marshal the resources to have a future. As G. K. Chesterton said to the church of his day, if you like the look of a fencepost and want to preserve it as it is, you must repaint the post every year. No faithful church is maintained without constant reformation, and no reformation has ever occurred without Spirit-induced preaching and leadership that inevitably produces discomfort in the people and in their leader.

A courageous pastoral leader, in service to the needs of the church,

* connects the congregation to its pain;
* helps it conceive of its possibilities;

* challenges it to step out of its current attitudes that rob it of a future;
* accompanies the organization through the resulting chaos; and
* supports the reframing and learning that's required for transformation.

Preaching can be an indispensable contributor to each of these leadership tasks.

The pain that an organization needs to face is discomfort that comes from an admission of the discrepancy between the way things currently are and the way things could be. Ye shall know the truth, and it will hurt. There can be no change without the introduction of conscious discomfort into the system. The leader works to give the organization the option either to deny or to undertake the work that's required to have a different future than the one to which the organization fears it is fated. Because truth-telling is a major work of leadership required in our day, we preachers are uniquely equipped to lead; preaching tells the truth about God.

The leader induces pain as a necessary, unavoidable prelude to the possibility of the achievement of something better in the conviction that God really wants us to succeed at this work. False hopes and easy answers are unfaithful attempts to have a future on our own: work more sincerely and feverishly at what we did in the past, do what we've always done, and perhaps we can fashion a future without having to ask God for help.

These truths of leadership ought to be unsurprising to those of us who must preach every Sunday. Preachers routinely dare to disturb by saying, in effect, "Here's a word you have been avoiding all week," or "We need to have an honest conversation," or

"Can you believe that Jesus would say something like this to people like us?"

In preparing to move from the biblical text to a sermon, I have found that it's a good interpretive principle to look for the tension in the text, to focus upon the trouble, the point of pain. The tension between the congregation and the text can be a preacher's ally. Trouble draws our listeners to question, to engage, and infuses energy into our proclamation.

I accompanied a group of church folks on a work team to clean up after Hurricane Katrina. For my sermon that Sunday I reached for an obvious text, Mark 6—Jesus coming to his disciples in the storm:

> We have just been through a terrible storm. Many of our churches, parsonages, and church facilities have been destroyed. Yet even amid the devastation it's good to know that Jesus comes to his followers in the storm and speaks, reassuring them, offering them peace. Sort of like what Jesus is doing for us during our time of need today. Right?
>
> Mark says that "Jesus made his disciples get into a boat and go ahead to the other side of the lake, toward Bethsaida, while he dismissed the crowd.
>
> "After saying good-bye to them, Jesus went up onto a mountain to pray. Evening came and the boat was in the middle of the lake, but he was alone on the land. He saw his disciples struggling. They were trying to row forward, but the wind was blowing against them. Very early in the morning, he came to them, walking on the lake. He intended to pass by them. When they saw him walking on the lake, they thought he was a ghost and

they screamed. Seeing him was terrifying to all of them. Just then he spoke to them, 'Be encouraged! It's me. Don't be afraid'" (Mark 6:45–50).

Jesus "made his disciples get in the boat" (a midnight sail in the storm was his idea, not ours) while he went off to pray. That's strange, considering the gathering tempest. But when Jesus "saw his disciples struggling" with the wind against them, "he came to them." That's what Jesus does. In the midst of the storm, he comes to us. Many of you can testify that when the sky is dark, when the storms of life are raging, Jesus comes to us and stands by us.

But this time through this beloved text I received a jolt, noticing a detail in the story I had never noted: "He intended to pass by them." *What?*

"Jesus, we're going down! Come save us!"

And Jesus, just out on the waves for a stroll, intending to go somewhere else important, interrupts his journey, stops, hears, and responds.

Intended to pass them by? What's that supposed to mean?

I couldn't shake the question "Can it be that Jesus has more important work than speaking to and rescuing his own followers?" Do you mean that Jesus's mission is greater and more expansive than our church in our time of need?[6]

I was on my way to an unexpected sermon. I had intended to lead by offering the church rather conventional pastoral reassurance: Jesus comes to us in the storm. Instead, after being smacked by verse 48, I had a different sort of leadership to offer.

Jesus comes to his people in the middle of our storms, yet his saving work is not limited to us. To be the church is to deal with our pain and tragedy but at the same time to be pushed to feel and to respond to someone else's pain outside the bounds of the church. Jesus loves us enough to call us to get out of the boat and venture forth with him into the storm, and then trusts us to accompany him on a mission that doesn't end in the boat. The boat (the *navis*, an ancient symbol for the church) is not Jesus's sole concern.

Be honest: sometimes the leadership pain that must be endured is personal. It's often tough to get a congregation to move or think outside the box in which it comfortably lives because we pastors are also in the box. It's easier for me to lead in the same way that worked for me in the last congregation than to refashion myself. I'm more comfortable leading in the ways in which I'm already equipped rather than in exploring new patterns of leadership.

I watched a pastor, during his first week in his new parish, tell the church council that he planned to "visit all of our older, homebound members during my first couple of weeks. I hear that many of them are feeling neglected."

"Why?" asked a layperson. "That's visitation that we ought to be doing. Not you."

"What would you suggest that your new pastor should be doing?" I asked.

"Why doesn't he have a face-to-face with every person related to this congregation who is under thirty? That would send a signal to the membership about priorities," replied the layperson. "He can do that in less than a week since we don't have many younger members."

Let's be honest: sometimes we preachers perform ministry like visitation of the elderly because that's the age group with whom we are most comfortable.

Internal maintenance is rewarded. Organizations do not want their leaders to undertake difficult work because it causes pain, even if that difficult work is necessary for the future of the organization. Churches tend to reward pastors for doing what they want done; they punish them for challenging their worldview. All systems favor self-protection and yearn for equilibrium, the church even more so. Yet confirmation of the listeners as they are is not effective leadership or faithful preaching. Whether they listen or refuse to listen (Ezek 2:5)—acceptance of the message by the listeners has never been the supreme test of Christian communication.

Empathy

How many of us went into the ministry in order to hurt people? We enjoy thinking of ourselves as peacemakers and reconcilers. Trouble is, Jesus Christ embodied not only love but also truth; there's no way to work for him without also being willing to risk contention and division in Jesus's name.

In a sermon on Numbers 13, Joshua's sending of the spies to reconnoiter Canaan, I thought I'd connect the text with our congregation's challenges of finding ourselves in a racially changing neighborhood:

> At last encamped upon the threshold of the Promised Land, two sets of spies were sent out to snoop around and then report back to the Israelites. The two groups

returned with a majority report and a minority report. The majority assessment was bleak: "The land looks dangerous. Compared with those fierce giants, we looked like grasshoppers. Let's go back to Egypt!"

The minority report was more optimistic: "Though there will be challenges, the land is lush and fertile. We can take it. God is with us. Let's go!"

Our congregation finds itself in a changed situation. The neighborhood that built this church, the people and place where we thrived, has slipped away from us. Are we on the threshold of the end of our congregation? Look at the numbers. Looks bleak. Huge challenges lie before us—giants; are they insurmountable?

Our neighborhood has changed. People who don't look like us are moving in, transforming our context, bringing neighborhood renewal. Our church did not initiate this changed situation, but now we must face it. We're right in thinking that our changed context requires us to change. Can we? Is it possible to see these contextual changes as a God-given opportunity?

New folks are moving in because they have found our neighborhood a great place to raise their families. Maybe, just maybe, they are moving in because God put them up to it. Perhaps these changes are a God-wrought, God-given opportunity to give our church a future. It won't be the same church we've known and loved, and that's kind of scary. But in a way, it's also exciting.

This morning, as we stand on the threshold of a new century, seeing the changes right here in our own backyard, whose version of our future will we believe?

Part of me listens to the "Back to Egypt Committee," the fearful naysayers who say, "On guard! This could be dangerous! We don't have the money or the people to match the giant problems facing us!"

But there's another part of me, maybe the best part, that hears God saying to us, "You are my church, the place from which I plan to do some of my best work among you and your new neighbors. Your new neighbors, whom you have yet to meet, are my people. I've got plans for you! Don't be afraid! Let's go!"[7]

When a pastor preaches, the word of God is articulated by one who knows the people and who is known by them. The word arises out of a shared condition. It takes courage to stand with a congregation that is having to ask painful questions: even more courage is required to speak the truth to people one has learned to love. The loving pastor has got to find a way to be the truthful preacher.

Reinhold Niebuhr said he had always thought that preachers were cowards in the pulpit because they feared that, if they spoke out on controversial issues, they would be fired. But when he became a pastor embedded in a congregation, Niebuhr discovered how difficult it is to speak the truth to people one has learned to love. A pastor gets a front-row seat from which to observe the misery that grips many people's lives of quiet desperation. The last thing a pastor wants is to preach something that makes people more miserable.

So the pastor trims the sermon to be safe and soothing, not out of fear of the congregation but out of love. Empathy kills more courageous sermons than does fear.

One of my colleagues asked my Introduction to Ordained Leadership class, "What is the most important thing pastors offer congregations?"

A dear, sweet seminarian replied, "Just be present with people—listen, love, and be with them."

"That's not good enough," snapped back the professor of pastoral care. "You must have the courage to be a *Christian* caregiver. Individuals and congregations can't get better unless somebody cares enough to help them hear and to enable them to respond to the facts. Placid 'presence' has too little impact on their need and too little in common with the gospel of Jesus Christ."

Rabbi Edwin Friedman always contended that empathy was the great enemy of pastoral leadership: pastoral self-protection and failure of nerve disguised as shielding others from pain. While empathy, being sensitive to and engaged by the suffering and pain of others, is part of the pastoral vocation, undisciplined empathy, without theological constraint, leads us away from our originating purpose and into a paralyzing failure of nerve. Friedman charges that "the introduction of . . . 'empathy' into family, institutional, and community meetings" is "an effort to induce a failure of nerve among its leadership."[8]

My first autumn as a bishop, a wise pastor told me, "You are a gift to us. But I worry that you will grow to like us, to befriend us, to feel sorry for us and, as you do, you will become less effective in helping us. Be careful! We Alabamians will charm you into complete ineffectiveness."[9]

My colleague Christopher Beeley says, "Contrary to what many think, the mark of humility in a Christian pastor is not low self-esteem or weak personality. Effective pastoral leadership requires much confidence and a comfort with exercising authority in people's lives."[10] For some time now it has been popular for clergy to refer to themselves as "servant leaders." The peculiar service *Christian* leaders render is not servility to the demands of the congregation but rather the courageous authority to push the church beyond being an internally caring and empathetic group of people to being disciples who courageously lay their personal trials and tribulations aside (a virtually un-American thing to do) in order to be in mission with Jesus.

Bishop Janice Huie has criticized the "excessive caregiving" in our seminaries—with extensive networks of student care and support—as creating an over-empathetic ethos that creates dependency and encourages wounded people to see their personal wounds as contributing to their ministry rather than to see how it is possible to be courageous leaders even when one has hurts and damage.

When empathy is unchecked, people expend energy on socializing, attending to one another in the organization, putting great stress upon the maintenance of relationships at all cost. The communal side is rewarded—people feel cared for and expect the organization to be a haven from the more painful aspects of their lives. Mutual comfort and care become the defining purpose of the congregation. The neediest, most vulnerable people set the tone for the congregation and exercise power and influence over the pastor's leadership.

Here's the rub: there is no way for this beloved, caring, internally empathetic organization to survive if it cannot find a way to lay aside its empathy and truthfully to face painful realities, to ask wounded people to step up and join in the mission of the church, and to move forward with a purpose larger than mutual care. Churches must go beyond caring empathy to engagement in risky mission. No way to do that without the courage to choose mission over relationship, and there's no way to do that without bold mission leader-preachers.

We pastors sometimes respond to organizational stresses by giving preference to empathy for individuals rather than to organizational leadership because empathy fits our personal skill set. Empathy is easier, requiring less courageous work.

I can testify from personal experience that when pastoral leaders focus upon their weakest, most needy members rather than spending time developing the strengths of their healthier members, the weaker members sabotage their leaders and regress, calling you cruel, autocratic, unfeeling, and uncaring. Friedman says that when they call you these names, "there is a good chance you're going in the right direction."[11] If you must empathize, make sure the chief object of your concern is the plight of the congregation, rather than allowing your ministry to be consumed with the pain of needy and demanding individuals.

Better said, we need to empathize with the right people. Rather than focus upon the older church member who refuses to change and who demands much of your attention, work instead with the older members whose children have abandoned the congregation because they decided it would never change. I am all for older-adult ministry, a growing field with the aging of mainline Protestantism. I have even written a book on the subject of ministry with and for older adults.[12] But it is a sad perversion when older-adult ministry keeps a church from having a future and excludes younger generations from confrontation by the claims of Christ. Pastors must find a way not to spend most of our time with our most damaged people so that we can have the energy to develop those people to whom God has given the gifts to help the congregation toward a vital future.

Rather than focus upon the people who threaten to leave unless we bow to their will and stop putting the congregation in pain, we should focus on all those who have given up hope for their church becoming relevant to the demands of discipleship in this age.

Fortunately, the skills required to preach the gospel without flinching are marvelously transferable to the demands of leading congregational embodiment of the gospel.

Some years ago I struggled with how to broach the subject of sexual abuse in a sermon (David and Bathsheba was my text). I worried that the issue might be too painful for some of my church's more sensitive ears.

I preached the sermon. The next week four women from the congregation made appointments to tell me their stories of being abused by men.

"I've spent years in therapy," said one, "but to have those words bounce off the walls of our church, to have this subject laid upon the altar, has been most therapeutically helpful."

As a preacher, rather than have my voice stifled by empathy with those who might be made uncomfortable by my words, I need to muster empathy for all those who are suffering because they never hear in a sermon the word they are dying to hear.

Good leaders must have a high tolerance for pain; sometimes the pain that's most painful is my own. Much of the work I do is done simply because it's less painful than the work the church needs me to do. I therefore believe that preaching is the most formative and determinative of pastoral duties, the fount from which all theologically driven leadership flows. If we can habitually stand in the pulpit and tell the truth of Jeremiah or Jesus, caring more about serving the truth rather than servility to the adoration of our congregation, we may be able to be leaders who tell our congregations the truth they've been evading and thereby enable them to engage in the adventure they've been missing.

Kierkegaard noted that many bright people in his age had blessed the world with labor-saving devices that made life easier. He declared that he would take a different path, the way of the Crucified: he would become a preacher devoted to making everyone's life more difficult.

What a wonderful way to make a living!

3

Leading as Teaching

Although Joe was a pastor of a predominately white, upper middle-class congregation, he had spent much of his ministry engaged in social justice. After an incident of racial violence in his city, Joe preached a series of three sermons in which he examined America's racial divide in a Christian way. He braced himself for possible congregational pushback in response to his bold sermons.

Joe was disappointed. Although the congregation had not openly rejected his sermons, their lack of response was deafening. At the church board meeting, Joe couldn't hold back his resentment.

"This church can't face the truth about America's greatest sin," he told them.

One of the oldest members of the board responded to Joe's outburst by asking, "Pastor Joe, how many extended conversations or significant encounters have you had with someone of another race this week?"

"I spend most of my time with you, and you look just like me," Joe laughed nervously.

She turned to her fellow board members and asked, "How many of you have had a significant interaction with someone of another race in the past week?"

When two-thirds of the board members raised their hands, she said with a smile, "Joe, you need to get out more. If you are going to help us solve our race problem, you need to be sure you take advantage of the work God is already doing among us right here in this church."

Who preached to whom in that exchange?

In order to be leaders who enable people to reframe, reconsider, and reimagine, preachers must be learners alongside the congregation. Sometimes, as in Pastor Joe's case, the chief learner is the pastor.

Adaptive Leadership

In *The Practice of Adaptive Leadership,* Ron Heifetz famously defined leadership as educational, adaptive work that enables systems to adapt by mobilizing people to rethink and then to tackle organizational problems. An adaptive leader studies the specifics of the leadership context and then addresses the conflicts between the values people say they hold and the reality they face. Rather than suppress conflict, the adaptive leader is courageous enough sometimes to instigate though always to orchestrate conflict so that people may learn new ways of thinking and acting.

Curiosity and the willingness to learn, to grow, to be surprised, and to be flexible are therefore essential attributes for adaptive leaders. (Duplicate that list also as "Qualities Required for the Production of an Interesting Sermon.")

In his book on leading nonprofit organizations, Peter Drucker says that the way to develop people as leaders who are learners is to enlist them to be teachers.[1] When the needs of my inner-city congregation forced me to teach them some of the principles and practices of church growth, I learned more than my students. The pastor who models being a constant learner is the pastor who helps the entire congregation become a body of explorers, experimenters, and mutual students. We're in a situation in which we cannot simply try harder to do the same things; we must change our concepts of why we're doing what we're doing, so the church must be a community of learners and teachers.

The primary way that the Christian life is formed and sustained, learns and teaches, is by listening to sermons. Both Luther and Calvin reclaimed the Christian faith as an auditory, acoustical phenomenon. "The ears alone are the organ of the Christian," said Luther.[2] Preaching is not only the free speech of the church, our way of bringing to speech the odd, true story that is called "gospel," the story of our justification to God through the words and work of Christ. Preaching is also formative upon those who hear, God's way of sanctifying in the truth those who listen for God in Jesus Christ (John 17:17).

Yet the ability to listen and to learn from a sermon is not innate. Contemporary culture indoctrinates us to listen solely to our own psyches, the voice of our alleged "conscience," or the imperial demands of the crowd, to governmental press releases, or the slick slogans of advertising. The modern world holds the governmentally sanctioned and subsidized belief that the only voices worth listening to are self-derived. The government has found that lone individuals are easier to manage than those who expect to be addressed by someone outside their own egos.

In this cultural context the faithful hearing of sermons is bound to seem unnatural and abnormal. A consumer economy trades by way of distraction. Advertising drowns out more subtle, complex communication. Discourse becomes reduced to snappy snippets, slogans and proverbs, texting. Prose that claims to be easily accessible by speaking straightforwardly on the basis of simple "facts" is privileged over metaphorical, poetic speech. In such a cultural climate, Christian preaching is charged with being authoritarian, archaic, obtuse, one-way communication; the dominant voices of the state, the economy, and the psyche are intolerant of rival ways of characterizing reality.

Therefore, it takes time for Christians to learn to be appropriately attentive to preaching. An array of practices is required, few of which are innate and none of which are supported by the dominant culture. A pressing task for today's church—particularly in a North American culture that is in active, though not always evident, rebellion against submission to the word of God—is inculcation of the practices required to listen to a sermon without wanting to kill the preacher (Luke 4). In short, people must be trained to listen to a sermon like Christians.

Walter Brueggemann says the church "is not self-generated, but understands itself in terms of a special authorization in a script available for steady and regular, attentive reiteration."[3] Like Israel, the church is gathered, not as the world gathers, on the basis of race, gender, nation, or class. The words of Scripture are not spoken merely in order to elicit agreement or noble feelings among the hearers, but rather to form and reform the hearers. It is the nature of Scripture to be formative, to want power over our lives, to absorb our world into the biblical world, to tune our ears to receive the truth of Jesus Christ.

An aspect of every preacher's leadership is helping people to listen expectantly, obediently, and faithfully. Every preacher preaches in the conviction that the gospel is able to gather the listeners whom the reign of God requires. God not only calls people to preach to God's people but also provides a congregation enabled to hear a theme so strange and wonderful, a word so demanding and odd as the good news of Jesus Christ. As Martin Luther reassured preachers of his day, God will not only give them words to preach but "will surely also supply and send listeners who will take this instruction to heart."[4]

It takes time and training to learn how to talk and to listen like Christians:

Faithful Christian preaching is biblical—sermons talk about what Scripture talks about in the ways that Scripture talks. Christians are those who, at least on a weekly basis, bend their lives toward the living, God-breathed, all-consuming word of God that demands to have authority over all of life. In the debate over whether or not we need more topical sermons and less lectionary-based preaching, for a church in great need of the theological rationale and authorization for the church, what we need is more *biblical* preaching; preaching formed by the substance, manner, and intent of Scripture.

People must expect to be surprised that God's ways are not our ways (Isa 55:9). Part of the adventure of Christian believing is the joy of being corrected by a sermon. Preaching is the bold, risky speaking of God's truth, not merely comfortable, deferential confirmation of our truths. Conversion, transformation of heart and mind, is a normal, expected aspect of interactions with Jesus

Christ. Therefore, it is not enough simply to respond to a sermon by asking oneself, "Do I agree with this?" or "Is this congruent with what I have always assumed?" Rather, faithful listening requires questions like "How must my life change in order to be better conformed to this truth?" "How would our congregation need to be different to be more clearly God's church?"

In listening to a sermon, our life may be caught up into purposes grander and more dangerous than our personal projects, namely a life commandeered by God. Preaching is not only the explication of a biblical text but also the text's application. Every biblical text tends to imply an imperative, moving naturally from proclamation to praxis. To listen to a sermon is to place oneself at risk of a potential summons, a vocation. Jesus rarely asks, "Do you agree?" More typical is his invitation, "Follow me!" Preaching means to "equip the saints for the work of ministry" (Eph 4:12, NRSV). Listening to sermons would be a harmless activity were it not for Christians' well-founded anticipation that God might use a sermon to call our names.

There is always the supposition that a sermon could disrupt my received world by verbally rendering the coming kingdom of God. A primary mode of Jesus's communication was parable—short, disarming, dislocating stories, often without neat conclusions, relating to everyday life yet also mysterious, opaque, and befuddling. When Jesus spoke of God's realm, he usually did so in parables, analogously, as if there were little about the kingdom of heaven that was self-evident or obvious, particularly to those of us more accustomed to living by the values of the kingdoms of this world. Confusion and consternation are expected byproducts of faithful preaching. True, Jesus said that the truth would make us free (John 8:32), but most lifetime listeners to sermons would add that the truth often makes one miserable before setting one free. In such painful attentiveness to the truth about God is our salvation. If you hear a sermon and respond, "Yes, that's what I've always thought," listen again; you probably heard it wrong.

To listen faithfully to a Christian sermon calls for a willingness not to receive an immediate, practical, personal pay-off. Scripture always and everywhere speaks primarily about God and only secondarily, and then often derivatively, about us. Our first reason for being in worship is to focus upon the God who, in Jesus Christ, has risked focusing upon us. We are therefore not present in worship first of all to receive our list of helpful hints for easier living, principles for a more purpose-driven life, motivation to a higher ethic, or keys to personal happiness. Sometimes we do receive such gifts from a sermon, but they are not the main point. The main point is the worship, adoration, praise, and submission to the God who has spoken to us. An always useful God and an instantly applicable sermon are often signs of idolatry, making ourselves and our own endeavors more significant than the Trinity. Moralism from the pulpit, presenting the gospel as human obligation rather than a divinely bestowed gift, something the listener is to think, feel, or do, is usually an indication that the preacher has jumped too quickly to the "What's in this for me?" rather than first to ask the more pressing and faithful "Is there any word from the Lord?" (Jer 37:17 NRSV).

Faithful listening includes a patient willingness to have some sermons speak to others but not to you. The truth articulated in a given sermon may not be the truth for which you are in desperate need right now. Sometimes "love your neighbor" (Matt 19:19) means a humble willingness to allow a sermon to speak primarily to your neighbor and not to you. Be patient, give thanks to God that your neighbor heard something in the sermon that you did not, and come back next Sunday in expectation of a sermon that God may more directly address to you.

Speaking and listening like Christians calls for vulnerability to the mysterious comings and goings of the Holy Spirit. Grace, an essential requirement for hearing a sermon's truth, is not grace if it's predictable and programmed. Only God can speak of God. Faithful preaching requires the descent and intervention of the Holy Spirit in order for the word of God to be received. John Calvin noted how upon hearing the same sermon, "twenty receive it with ready obedience of faith while the rest hold it valueless, or laugh, or hiss, or loathe it."[5] Delivery of a sermon is the preacher's job; fostering receptivity to a sermon is the self-assigned task of the Holy Spirit. "So neither the one who plants nor the one who waters is anything, but only God who gives the growth" (1 Cor 3:7 NRSV). It is therefore customary in some churches to pray a Prayer for Illumination before the reading and the exposition of Scripture, asking the Holy Spirit to open our hearts and minds to the word. No sermon can be heard unaided and alone.

Preaching is a communal activity. A sermon is public speech. The gathered congregation, with people convened to hear and then to enact the word, is the natural habitat for the exposition of God's word. A sermon begins, rather than ends, with the preacher's last words, taking on a life of its own within the congregation's cares and concerns, as well as the determination of the people of God to be not only receptive but also obedient. The effects of sermons are cumulative, over a lifetime gradually drawing us out of ourselves and into the life of God. A sermon often waits to bear fruit in the lives of the faithful long after the sermon has been preached. Listening for the word is an activity that permeates all of the church's life as insights on the significance of the preached word are shared, corrected, challenged, and encouraged within the conversation and the living of the congregation.

A preacher who is pastor must care more for the right explanation of the word of God (2 Tim 2:15) than for the love or the ire of the congregation. Pastors must stir up in themselves a more passionate desire to be truthful than their typical pastoral longing to be popular. Though a pastor must love a congregation, a faithful pastor loves the word of God even more. Sermons become boring when preachers tingle the ears of the faithful (Jer 19:3 NRSV) rather than please a truth-telling God. Listeners ought to give the preacher encouragement, praising a preacher who tries to be courageous more highly than a preacher who, in sermons, wants merely to be kind. Some congregations get the equivocating, inconsequential, tedious, sentimental, and trite sermons they deserve.

Listening faithfully calls for a joyful submission to the language of Zion, learning how to use the peculiar speech of the church, rather than demanding that the preacher attempt to translate our faith into language that is more acceptable to the culture. Learning to listen to a sermon today is somewhat akin to learning French. In order to be Christian, one must learn how to use the language, calling all things by their proper names. What the world calls "mistake," "a lapse in judgment," the church teaches us to name "sin." Much that the world calls "creative" we label "idolatry." The world seeks "justice"; we are bold to attempt "love." A Christian is someone who knows how to use the speech that God has given us through Scripture and church rather than jettisoning that speech for talk that is designed by the world to keep the world's reality afloat.

Faithful sermon listeners find joy in a preacher who attempts on Sunday to help us pay attention to matters we try to avoid all week long. A faithful preacher beguiles us, through various homiletical stratagems, into being attentive to matters (sin, death, grace, righteousness, salvation) that we think are too painful or too overwhelming to consider. One reason we often have stained-glass windows or bare interiors in our churches is in order to lessen worldly distractions so that, in listening to a sermon, we are attentive to reality (the kingdom of God) and less concerned with the sham that is presented to us in daily life as "the real world." By God's grace, we can stand more truth and put up with more reality than we think. We find that our self-defenses against the word are unwarranted. Having been justified by grace, we enjoy the sanctification that comes through growing in grace by listening to the truth: "Speaking the truth in love, we must grow up in every way into him who is the head, into Christ" (Eph 4:15, NRSV). It takes guts to listen closely to a sermon, but in receiving the truth gladly, we discover that we are not as cowardly as we first presumed.

We relinquish our prerogative to talk about what we are obsessed with discussing (sex, family, security, health) and offer a docile willingness to engage in conversation with a living God, talking about what God wants to talk about. John Calvin spoke of Scripture as the "lens" that God gives us to view and review the world. A lens brings some things into focus that were previously overlooked and puts some things out of focus that we once considered all-important. Preaching can have similar optical effects.

As we have noted, adaptive work requires an educator, more specifically a storyteller. (A *preacher!*) We can act only within the world in which we live, and we can live only in a world we can see, and we can see only the world about which we can speak. Stories create worlds. The one who would change people must offer better stories.

When you are disappointed and frustrated by your congregation's situation, just remember: they didn't get in this fix without someone leading them there. They can get out only by someone leading them elsewhere. Why shouldn't that preacher be you?

Sometimes the most painful adaptive change required is in the leader. Even as we criticize the congregation for its lack of suppleness and innovation, we must be honest about our own desire to stick to our most comfortable leadership style that worked for us in the past.

Adaptation requires movement, transformation, change. Sometimes what looks like pushback and resistance is a call for further explanation, a request for more information. Never tire of explaining to the congregation your rationale for your leadership style and goals.

Far too many pastors are content with present arrangements, managing the church as it is rather than to stretch themselves and risk envisioning the church as God intends it to be. The prophetic critique of the temple priesthood in the Old Testament was based upon the prophets' belief that the priests were content merely to keep house, to manage the status quo, rather than being open and receptive to the movements of a living God. Because church leadership is leadership in service to a dynamic, synergistic God named Trinity, leadership in the name of Christ is called to risk being at the center of transformation.

A congregation's self-contentment, a false sense that they are already fulfilling the purposes and mission of the church, can be a pastor's greatest enemy. In order to cultivate a sense of urgency, the leader must figure out how to energize people by bringing them face-to-face with the truth of their situation.

Acts 15:1–35 shows a dispute within the early church over the status of Gentile Christians, where there was "no small dissension and debate" (Acts 15:2, NRSV). Peter urges an openness to the Gentiles, citing his own experience (in Acts 10:1–11:18) of the way in which God "[makes] no distinction" between Jew and Gentile (Acts 15:9). James, on the other hand, quotes scriptural precedent (Amos 9:11–12). After much debate, a compromise is reached and the church officially moves to a new, transformed situation once James's proposal has the approval of "the apostles and the elders, along with the entire church" (Acts 15:22). I take this "Jerusalem Conference" as an example of biblical adaptive and transformative leadership.

Lest we think of the church as intransigent and terrified by change, church history ought to remind us that, historically viewed, the church is one of the most adaptable, supple organizations ever. Our history shows a remarkable ability to form and reform. Could we say that one of the invigorating aspects of being a Christian leader is that we get to serve in a time of multiple opportunities for ecclesial adaptation?

Some of our best reformations have been due not simply to changed political or cultural circumstances, nor to visionary leaders, but rather to God, the agent of change. We are less in control of our future than we like to believe. We gather information, plan, and lead, but so does God. God is free to bless or not bless our leadership initiatives. Is that why God's agency is rarely acknowledged, even in allegedly Christian leadership books?

The countercultural quality of the gospel requires leadership that is willing to be a means of constant conversion, ever willing to stand in that tension between the end of an old world and the beginning of a new, ready to acknowledge God's free, uncontrollable agency without being paralyzed, ever reformed and reforming. Thus Heifetz distinguishes between leadership that merely manipulates "the community to follow the leaders' vision" and leadership that "influences the community to face its problems."[6]

Living systems thrive by figuring out how to adapt by taking the best of their past and carrying it with them into the future through experimentation and invention. Systems crave homeostasis and stability, so they must learn how to call forth diverse resources within the organization that produce displacement and rearrangement of some of the organization's past practices without forsaking its core character.

That's why Greg Jones, dean of Duke Divinity School, tells seminarians that they must learn how to be "traditioned innovators." A Christian leader who "has been trained as a disciple for the kingdom of heaven is like the head of a household who brings old and new things out of their treasure chest" (Matt 13:52).

Here are some examples of "traditioned innovation," adaptive leadership in a sermon: "You have heard that it was said to those who lived long ago, *Don't commit murder,* and all who commit murder will be in danger of judgment. But I say to you that everyone who is angry with their brother or sister will be in danger of judgment" (Matt 5:21–22). "You have heard that it was said, *You must love your neighbor* and hate your enemy. But I say to you, love your enemies and pray for those who harass you so that you will be acting as children of your Father who is in heaven. He makes the sun rise on both the evil and the good and sends rain on both the righteous and the unrighteous" (Matt 5:43–45).

Acts 15 portrays leadership in the early church as a process of adapting to the truth of Jesus Christ. Peter helped the church reframe its questions, moving from "It's not right for these gentiles to be claiming a part in our Messiah's realm," to "If then God gave them the same gift that God gave us when we believed in the Lord Jesus Christ, who are we to hinder God?"

Reframed, they were able to praise God and stride into a new reality: "So then God has enabled Gentiles to change their hearts and lives so that they might have new life" (Acts 11:18).

Because deep transformation/adaptation is something that God does, one of the challenges of church leadership is to preach the sort of sermons and to convene the sort of meetings that give God room to work in changing people.

Refusing to be either trapped or driven by followers' conventional expectations, the transformational leader calls followers to a larger purpose, a higher moral commitment, enabling both the organization and its members to be transformed. Progress requires a leader willing to risk disapproval and even rejection in the interest of transformation.

The church must change, not so much to invent new ways of doing things but rather to reclaim the church's core identity and mission. Fortunately, nurturance of core identity and mission are two major purposes for preaching.

Thus I advise young seminarians, "Take care not to push people too far in what you say in a sermon. On the other hand, always risk taking them as far as they need to go."

Pastors organize, convene, and orchestrate the congregation in its ministry, but sometimes the pastor must risk going ahead of the congregation in the pulpit, knowing that few congregations will outpace what their pastor is able to say in a sermon.

When Willie Earle was lynched after a mob took him from the Pickens, South Carolina, jail in February of 1947, the young Methodist preacher in town, Hawley Lynn, immediately convened a meeting of the town's church leaders for the purpose of condemning the lynching. When the meeting ended in angry turmoil, Hawley was advised to let the matter drop.

He went back to his parsonage and began a sermon based on texts from Amos and Acts. In his sermon the next Sunday, "Who Lynched Willie Earle?," Hawley began by thanking his congregation for their wonderful practice of Methodist "freedom of the pulpit." This ingratiating introduction should have signaled to them that a prophetic sermon was about to be delivered.

"Who lynched Willie Earle?" asked Hawley. "We all know who lynched him—'men from another county.'" A dozen of the lynchers had already signed confessions; their names were published in the local paper for all to see. Hawley paused for effect, then asked, "Who lynched Willie Earle? *We did!*" Then Hawley launched into a jeremiad against the sin of racial segregation and South Carolina's denial of the rights of African Americans, comparing the plight of the victim Jesus to that of racial minorities in the South, and ending in a rousing appeal to the congregation to witness to the love of Christ, who challenges our inbred racism.[7]

Faithful sermons require risk-taking preachers because a sermon is not merely a statement about where the congregation is, but an inspired witness to where God is calling the congregation to be.

The Formation of the Adaptive Leader

The changed and ever-changing cultural context of the church in North America requires most of us clergy to adapt in order to be adaptive leaders. The preparation and expectation for leadership that we received in seminary, if any, must be transformed. Heifetz lists seven practical suggestions for bearing the responsibility that comes from adaptive leadership (which I've adapted for the church from chapters 4–7 of Heifetz's *The Practice of Adaptive Leadership*):

✳ Get on the balcony (find ways to gain distance from the congregation's situation in order to obtain perspective [like up in the pulpit?]).

✳ Distinguish yourself (your personal needs and aspirations) from the leadership role you fulfill in service to the church.

✳ Externalize and depersonalize conflict (this is not about you, nor is congregational response to your leadership a referendum on your success as a pastor).

✳ Look for partners and allies in order to solve the problem (delegating and empowering the baptized are your main task, not undertaking the work yourself).

✳ Listen, inviting outsiders' points of view (sometimes your critics are right and those who oppose a course of action can be enlisted as allies once their criticisms are heard).

✳ Seek a sanctuary where you can detach from the heat of the conflict and gain the input of a coach or mentor (most of the work that God gives pastors cannot be done alone). Get a wise counselor who can be trusted to help, who is willing to take time to get to know your strengths and weaknesses, and who is willing to be in a sustained relationship with you to help you grow in your leadership.

✳ Preserve a sense of purpose that is constantly defined and reiterated (be sure you know "Why?" before you ask "Where?"). Keep refurbishing your sense of vocation and your commitment to the theological purposes of the church and its ministry.

Here's a Heifetz point that caused me consternation: *Adaptive change takes time.* Heifetz says that we must "give the work back to people, but at a rate they can stand."[8] Adaptive change requires time for people to rethink their situation, to come to terms with the truth about their condition, and then to gain confidence that God has given what their church needs to thrive.

Congregations expect new pastors to quickly and painlessly solve their problems—as *they* define their problems. They tend to define the condition they're in ("We are an aging congregation") as a problem to be fixed by their pastor ("You must attract younger members"). If (as I do) the pastor enjoys being a problem-solver, then the new pastor dives in to show the congregation that she is a much better fixer than the previous pastor, accepting the congregation's definition of the problem as accurate. Trouble is, the conception that the pastor is the problem-solver sidetracks the most important and badly needed gift that the pastor has to offer the congregation: teaching, reframing, and confronting the truth—which, though it may be painful, is essential in order to embrace and live into realistic possibility.

I'm impatient (that is, I like to control other people's time). I first discovered my impatience not as a leader but as a preacher. Eugene Lowry's books on the sermon as the movement of narrative through time showed me that I tended to give away my sermon's "point" too soon, using a key sermon illustration too early in the sermon and rushing my listeners to end their listening too early.[9] Sometimes a listener's reception of a sermon occurs weeks or months after the sermon. Good preachers must be in love with planting the seed and patient in waiting for the harvest. The patience required to preach and to wait for response to a sermon can be salubrious training for the impatient leaders among us.

The Ministry of Administration

Many leadership books play off *management* against *leadership*, lamenting a preponderance of bean-counter managers and paper-shuffling administrators when what we need are bold, visionary leaders. Leadership sounds noble and courageous; management smacks of small-mindedness.

Pastors can't afford to choose between being a leader or a manager. We must be good at "big picture" leadership tasks that help a congregation know where it ought to go, and also be good at the daily, hands-on administrative tasks that move us in that direction. If we can't adequately perform both tasks, then it's our obligation to seek help from laity whom God has equipped for these essential ministries. Gil Rendle says that while good leaders must find opportunities to climb out of the day-to-day grind of congregational life in order to take the long view, good managers accompany the organization into the threatening chaos that change requires: "Managers help organizations do things right; leaders help organizations do right things."[10]

New pastors often complain that seminary gave them many good ideas but little training in how to transform those ideas into concrete reality. "I know what to do but haven't a clue how to do it," said one young pastor. That statement is usually a commentary on a lack of administrative expertise. While there are strong links between preaching and leading, it's important to note that the leadership responsibilities of teaching, rethinking, and adapting are not the sole leadership tasks of the pastor. There must be movement from good intentions and fitting goals to the practical work that must occur to fulfill those intentions. Pastors not only lead by articulating a vision, reframing the congregation's problems, and nurturing the theological purpose of the church and its ministry; we also lead through competent, efficient, hands-on administration.

In a sermon series on racism and the Christian faith, Pastor Tom Berlin walks his congregation through a concise but brutally truthful history of racism in the laws and society of twentieth-century America. Taking Acts 15 as his text, he titled his sermon "Trouble in Paradise."

Early in his sermon, Tom makes a scriptural claim: "The gospel has a lot to do with equity and inequity, justice and injustice, who's in and who's out. Paul took on Peter, the face of the church, because he believed that this topic of race was foundational to the truth of the gospel itself."

Not content to give a sweeping history of race in America or just to exegete Acts 15, Tom ends his sermon with a concrete call to action:

> What am I asking you to do?
>
> Educate yourself—read an article or a book—I'll give you ideas in this week's e-note or you can do it for yourself.
>
> Be intentional about conversations. Ask people about their experiences and families, how they grew up. When you do, listen and fight the urge to correct or fix things when you feel uncomfortable.
>
> Sign up for "Dinner for 8." [Dinner for 8 was a series of weekly church dinners where a racially diverse group of eight people per table discussed eight questions about race and the Christian faith.]

Berlin shows pastoral leadership from the pulpit at its best as concrete, active embodiment of the dictates of Scripture.

John Kotter's seminal book, *Leading Change*,[11] warns that strong leadership without good management gets an organization nowhere, contending that leadership and management are two "distinctive and complementary systems of action."

Leadership is about vision, overall direction, goals and ends. It's necessary for organizational transformation. However, management is required for effective operation and execution. Kotter defines management as "coping with complexity." Churches, even relatively small congregations, can be surprisingly complex organisms with many different, often competing components. Somebody has to be the glue that holds things together, the person who is not overwhelmed by the complexity, and the one who says, "First, let's do this; next, . . ."

An organization moves forward by means of more than high visions and good intentions; at some point someone must take responsibility for seeing that things get done. Good management increases an organization's capacity to move forward by developing necessary structures, evaluating and planning events and processes, getting the right staff in place, holding people accountable, rewarding people who contribute, and exiting those from leadership who detract from an institution's forward movement.[12]

Leadership helps people move in the same general direction by talking—motivating and inspiring. Management does the face-to-face, nitty-gritty work to engage in the difficult conversations required and the oversight of execution of ideas that enable an inspiring vision to become an operational reality. Managers push people through mechanisms of oversight and control. Leaders inspire people by energetically playing to people's basic need for achievement, a sense of belonging, recognition by others, and the power to live up to their highest ideals. Management values control and minimizes risk; leadership requires energy and, therefore, inspiration (literally "filled with spirit").

No grand vision is achieved, says Kotter, without "a burst of energy." Thus good leaders tend to be inspiring motivators; they know how to assess people's highest values and enhance those values. They invite others into decisions, without being captive to their opinions, and give them a sense that they have some control over their destiny. Yet they also make sure that inspired people don't become frustrated because nothing happens. Pastors don't have to be good at both leadership and management, but they must be good at finding others in the congregation who are.

By natural inclination and theological training, we pastors tend to be persons who enjoy ideas and abstractions; the leadership needs of the church in the present age demand that we also roll up our sleeves and administer and manage. Financial leadership of a congregation is not fulfilled by a series of good sermons on stewardship. Someone has to lead movement from great ideas to skillfully securing the right people to oversee the finances, setting up appropriate mechanisms for financial support, keeping track of receipts and disbursements, and maintaining systems of counting and accountability.

I'm a great advocate of having competent, experienced outside consultants and coaches study and then make recommendations for a congregation's future. At their best, outside consultants are teachers. Yet, adaptive challenges cannot be addressed merely by bringing in an expert to dictate what we ought to do, because adaptive solutions lie in the new attitudes, competencies, and coordination of the people who adapt corporate life to their new condition. The problem resides among the people who have been gathered by Christ; the solution lies with them too. Those of us in authority must orchestrate, equip, and coordinate people to do this hard work rather than try to fix the problem for them.

Good church administration begins with a pastor's recognition that administration is a necessary aspect of ministry. Whereas leaders help manage the change that needs to occur for the organization to thrive, administrators cope with the complexity of enlisting, training, commissioning, evaluating, and holding accountable people to undertake all the tasks that must be accomplished if the necessary change is to occur.

Leaders are "big picture" persons who get up on the balcony and look into the distance in order to help the congregation see where it ought to be going. Managers work on the ground making sure we are doing what we need to do in order to go where we believe God wants us to go. Pastors must be both leaders and managers.

The different but complementary tasks of administration and leadership are somewhat akin to what must occur on the way to a sermon. A sermon is more than a set of interesting ideas; a sermon is a particular arrangement of ideas that are presented orally. Homiletics is a supremely practical discipline. When I lead a workshop on preaching, before the day is done one of the participants is bound to ask, "This is all well and good but, Will, what are the steps you take in order to come up with a sermon?"

Because sermons involve not only what to say but also how to say it, we preachers are big on structure when it comes to planning a sermon. An unstructured sermon is incomprehensible. Decisions must be made by the preacher about what, when, and how to say something in the sermon, practical steps we follow on the journey toward a culminating response that is music to the preacher's ears: "Thanks! God spoke to me today in your sermon."

Yet, we preachers also know that when all our sermon design and construction is done, we are still utterly dependent upon the gift of the Holy Spirit in order for preaching to "work." We need to take some of that sense of dependency upon the Spirit into our administration of the church as well. Sometimes I fear that overly elaborate, rule-driven church structures are a defense against the disruptive incursions of the Holy Spirit. Although there's not much room for the promptings of the Holy Spirit, we are determined to keep the machinery cranking along anyhow. Do we pastors allow our lives to be consumed with committee meetings, paper shuffling, and machinery oiling in order to protect ourselves from undertaking the more threatening tasks of ministry?

When I'm consulting in a congregation and ask the lay leaders to tell me how they honestly feel about the work of their church, rarely do they complain about their pastor's lack of visionary leadership. More typically, they share their frustration with poorly run, long and meandering, unproductive meetings with no agenda, plans made but not executed, discussion of the same problems at meeting after meeting, little follow-up on decisions and initiatives from previous meetings, unclear lines of responsibility, unrealistic or vague goals, no evaluation, no accountability of effectiveness, and lack of a clear sense of direction. These complaints inevitably point to someone at the top who is trying to be a pastor without learning and executing good administration.

Jackson Carroll made a study of mainline congregations and found that 15 percent of the average pastor's week is spent administering the congregation's affairs and attending congregational meetings. Another 13 percent is spent training or equipping people for ministry. It's important to learn how to be an efficient administrator so we will get administration done quickly in order to have more time and energy for more demanding ministry—like preparing to preach. Protracted, excessive meetings can be a pastor's way of avoiding more difficult work, since meetings give the illusion that we are actually accomplishing something. No, a meeting is the administrative work we do to get ready for the work of ministry; meetings are not the work.

One of my early congregations passed a rule that no meeting could last longer than an hour. Attendance went up and people were more energized and engaged in the meetings. Better administration sometimes begins in setting goals that require us to set up the structures that in turn require us to be more efficient.

I secured the services of a coach to help me (that's my main recommendation for pastors who want to grow in administrative ability—get a coach). After following me around for a few days, looking over my shoulder as I led the congregation, among his recommendations (at least those that I am willing to share with you!), he advised the following:

* You are not good at remembering details; write it down!
* Never go into a meeting without a written agenda that is distributed to every person prior to the meeting. Ruthlessly keep the discussion tied and timed to the agenda.
* Whenever someone agrees to do a job, make sure they are given a specific date for completion. Put that date on your calendar for follow-up if they don't report back to you on their completion of the job.
* Don't add to busy people's workload without having them tell you what they will stop doing in order to perform well the new task that you lay upon them.

* Start meetings on time and always have an agreed-upon time to end.
* Ask lots of questions and allow the group time to come up with answers before suggesting answers of your own.
* No need for a face-to-face meeting when an email exchange would suffice.
* Recruit the right people for specific jobs rather than waiting for them to volunteer.
* If nobody volunteers, it may be a sign that the job is pointless.
* Keep church structure, the number of committees, the number of church officers to a bare minimum to get the job done.
* Don't take responsibility for some task until you are absolutely certain that God has not called someone else in the congregation to undertake this ministry.
* Don't wait for group consensus to initiate change that you are certain needs to be undertaken. Be prepared to ask for forgiveness rather than wait for approval.

I could go on.

In order to grow in your administrative and management ability, there's a good chance God has given you people within the congregation who can help you learn. Effective procedures for hiring church staff may not have been part of your seminary training, but good hiring practices are another day at the office for many of your laity. They can teach you.

We must do nothing, in our leadership and administration, to rob the laity of their baptismally bestowed obligation to be in mission with Jesus. I therefore think it a good idea for us preachers to view ourselves as the manager of a potentially winning baseball team rather than the team's star player. In every sermon, we ought to include some story or illustration that narrates some exemplary way some person (other than the preacher) has embodied the gospel. Such exemplification leads to identification and empowerment. The pastor partners with God to call people to ministry, constantly giving ministry away, modeling good leadership by not robbing them of their baptismally given ministries. We are not so much the leader of the congregation as we are the trainer, supporter, and evaluator of the lay leaders.

How curious for Acts, amid all the exciting work of the Holy Spirit, to give us this detailed account of the apostolic ministry of administration:

> During this time, as the disciples were increasing in numbers by leaps and bounds, hard feelings developed among the Greek-speaking believers—"Hellenists"— toward the Hebrew-speaking believers because their widows were being discriminated against in the daily food lines. So the Twelve called a meeting of the disciples. They said, "It wouldn't be right for us to abandon our responsibilities for preaching and teaching the Word of God to help with the care of the poor. So, friends, choose seven men from among you whom everyone trusts, men full of the Holy Spirit and good sense, and we'll assign them this task. Meanwhile, we'll stick to our assigned tasks of prayer and speaking God's Word." The congregation thought this was a great idea. They went ahead and chose—
>
> Stephen, a man full of faith and the Holy Spirit, Philip, Procorus, Nicanor, Timon, Parmenas, Nicolas, a convert from Antioch.

Then they presented them to the apostles. Praying, the apostles laid on hands and commissioned them for their task. (Acts 6:1–6, *The Message*)

The apostles designate seven to be deacons, not because the Twelve are too self-important to work the food line but rather because feeding the widows is too important a task for distracted, overworked teaching and preaching apostles to do poorly.

Pastor Anthony Robinson helpfully lists ten "rules of leadership" that are particularly applicable for pastors who, in service to Christ's mission, are called to administer change in order to help the congregation accomplish its mission:[13]

1. Give responsibility back. When a layperson says, "Somebody ought to be doing this," Robinson says he learned to say, "That sounds like just the thing God may be calling you to do." In our pastoral leadership, we must discipline ourselves not to take away the laity's baptismally bestowed ministry. (Preach on the vocation of all Christians at every baptism.)

2. Expect trouble. Too many pastors see themselves as peacemakers, reconcilers. Pastors like to be liked and enjoy pleasing people. Trouble is, conversion is inherently part of the Christian faith. The call for relinquishment of one belief and the embrace of another can produce conflict. People rarely give up power easily. Sometimes, the congregation is dependent upon the pastor to cause trouble in order to ignite needed changes.

(I vividly recall a morning after an unusually stormy board meeting. I sat in my study wondering what went wrong. Had I pushed too soon? Should I have been more patient? Ought I to have been more careful in my advocacy of a controversial position? Then I turned to the work at hand, preparation for next Sunday's sermon from the Gospel of Mark. As is typical of Mark, the text was a story of conflict. Jesus preached. The congregation reacted in anger and rejection. It was as if a light went on in my brain, as if a voice from the text asked, "Now, what about 'cross' do you find surprising? Jesus encountered trouble nearly every time he preached." The Holy Spirit interrogated me: "Are you a more skillful preacher than Jesus? Have you found a way to lead without getting hurt? If so, it's a shame Jesus didn't know what you know. He could have begun a seminar and avoided all that pain of Calvary.")

Trouble comes with the territory. Conflict is not a sign of leadership failure; failure to manage conflict is a sign of inability to be the sort of leader required by the gospel. Defeat is rarely an unmitigated setback, a total loss, but rather a lesson to be learned, a journey to be managed on the way to what must be done next to be more faithful to our vocation.

3. Value small steps. It is a virtue to have a long-range vision, but it is essential for the pastor to realize that one gets there by a series of many small steps. In today's fast-paced, ever-changing world, long-range planning may be a waste of time. Something inherent within the nature of the gospel values small things—the widow's two coins, the pearl of great price, the few seeds that fell upon good soil—small things that the world regards of low account. (As we have the one-to-one conversation, teach the only two children who showed up for Sunday school, visit the one sick person, or dutifully deliver a sermon to the faithful few, remember that the exodus from slavery began with one step.)

4. Plan. A poorly planned sermon is a poor sermon. If you do not know where you are going, almost any road will take you there. Laity complain about the wasted time and dissipated energy that result from having no wider vision for the congregation, no means of holding ourselves accountable, no way to

know when we have actually accomplished something and ought to celebrate. Though long-range planning may be inappropriate in an age when the church must be supple and adaptive, short-range planning helps keep a church on course, enables a pastor to prioritize pastoral time and to focus energies in a commonly conceived direction. (It takes longer to plan a sermon than to deliver it.)

5. Identify the vital few. Who are those who get things done? Who in the congregation can be counted on to make things happen? You may not be able to rely on the officially elected leaders in order to initiate transformation. Sometimes the function of traditional leadership structure is to preserve the status quo. Don't waste time vainly attempting to talk intransigent people into being innovative. Go with the few people whom God has given you who, by temperament and gifts, can be helpful in moving forward. Rid the church of pointless committees and unnecessary positions. Improve the few things you are already doing well rather than take on new tasks that might not go well. Don't tackle too many things at once; stick with the few things that are essential and possible. Give the congregation a few victories to celebrate rather than risk constantly being overwhelmed by defeats. (Usually, the best sermon editing is in deleting what we will not say this Sunday rather than in adding more material.)

6. Don't overvalue consensus. Pastors tend to want to bring everyone along with all congregational moves—a sure way to guarantee a lack of movement. Obdurate individuals, while they cannot be allowed to hold the congregation back from its necessary adaptive work, should be given the dignity to not approve of and not participate in every ministry of the church. Avoid putting everything to a vote. Sometimes we need to ask members who have grave reservations about some course of action to

trust those who want to move. Things can be evaluated later. If we wait until everyone is on board, we disempower those who are ready to take risks, and risk-takers are usually in short supply. There may even be rare, difficult times when a pastor must be willing to split a congregation, be willing to let dissident, stubborn members disaffiliate in order to give the congregation a future. Pastors are called to a ministry of reconciliation and peacemaking, yes. But in the present age we are also called to ministries of transformation, rebirth, and renewal. In order for something to be transformed, its old form must give way to the new, and that can be painful. The pain must be endured, expected, even welcomed, if there is to be new life. (No preacher expects everyone to receive God's word gladly.)

7. Count the yes votes. We sometimes worry more about those who are not yet ready to move or may never be ready to move than we worry about those who are bored, frustrated, and disheartened when too little takes too long to happen in the church. I confess that I tend, as a preacher, to hear the voices of the two sermon critics long after I have forgotten the praise of the dozen who liked my sermon. Sometimes we need to let the enthusiastic lay leaders go ahead, counting the yes votes. Rarely will a majority support a new ministry from the first, particularly if the new ministry requires risk. (Still, every preacher knows not to launch into a church building program if the vote is 52–48.)

8. Create a new working group for a new job. Established structures tend to protect the status quo. Established boards love to say no. If there is a new ministry to be done, you probably ought to create a new committee, composed of those who feel called to this work, to do the job. (Ask the established committees not to stand in the way of new movements within the

congregation, promising them an opportunity to help with later evaluation of the initiative.)

9. Change by addition, not subtraction. It is easier to get approval to begin a project than to kill an established ministry. Why mobilize the supporters of the established program against you by declaring it dead and ready for burial? Go ahead with new initiatives. If the new program succeeds, people will gradually rally around it. (People are more likely to let go of the old if they have something new to embrace.)

10. Be persistent. Change, no matter how obviously needed, inevitably provokes resistance. Resistance, particularly where the matter is our devotion to and service of God, can be deep and unrelenting. Constancy is one of the essential virtues for Christian ministry. Robinson advises, "Don't give up too soon." Studies indicate that it takes about five years before a pastor has gained the trust of a congregation to make significant, threatening change. For many women pastors, it seems to take even longer. Count on a couple more years before you see significant fruit. In a mobile society, where transiency is the norm, pastors must be in for the long haul if they are to be truly transformative leaders.

Congregations Go No Further Than Their Pastor Does

In visits to countless congregations, and in my own pastoral experience, I have come to the rather frightening conclusion that pastors are a decisive element in the vitality and mission of the church. To be sure, as we have said repeatedly, the pastor is not to assume responsibility for all ministry in the church. The baptized are the chief ministers in the name of Christ. Pastors lead through service rather than dominance. The Holy Spirit is the source of all ministry. Still, the pastor is decisive. The pastor's mood and attitude set the tone for the congregation, convey hope and energy to the people, hurt and heal, bind and release. The leadership and administrative skills that the pastor acquires set the boundaries for how far a congregation will be able to go. Sometimes, as a pastor, I wish it were not so, but it is.

What Jesus wants for the church must become incarnate in a pastor or, in my experience, it does not happen. Clergy work within a community. Clergy can't do everything by themselves— in fact, they do almost nothing by themselves; however, congregations rarely accomplish more than the courage, creativity, and capacity of their pastoral leaders.

A distinguished church-growth consultant, in a workshop on congregational development, spent more than an hour listing all the factors relevant to the vitality and growth of a congregation. Then he said ominously, "If the pastor's leadership is lacking, you can discount everything that I have listed on the board. If the pastor is an inadequate administrator and leader, none of the factors that I have listed make any difference."

I know that some large congregations divide the pastoral leadership by having a "preaching pastor" whose ministry is limited to the pulpit and an "executive pastor" who administers and manages the church. I've met pastors of less-than-large congregations who boast, "My ministry is delivering the word in preaching, and I leave running the church to my staff."

While there is much to be said for having someone trained and capable to handle the demanding tasks of leadership and the details of competent administration, it's important to note how administrative duties enrich and inform our preaching. We go to the ancient biblical text fresh from Thursday's disastrous evangelism committee meeting. We mount the pulpit not only with Matthew's Gospel but also amid congregational anxiety about this year's budget. Thus there is a greater chance of the text being in dialogue with our missional context, an increased likeliness that the sermon will touch down somewhere in the present moment, and that a sense of relevance and urgency will pervade our proclamation.

Leading, administering, and preaching—all three—are among the most significant gifts Christ gives his church.

4

Courage to Lead from the Pulpit

On a June night in 1974 I was ordained to preach by a denomination of over ten million members. The next morning, for the first time in history, my church began losing members. During my four decades of sermons, we've lost four million. As Stanley Hauerwas and I announced in *Resident Aliens*, the once comfortable alignment of church and culture that North American mainline Protestantism had worked to our advantage began unraveling. North American culture has made our congregations countercultural, salmon swimming against the stream, whether or not we wanted to be.

I doubt that our unfaithful preaching has led to denominational demise, though that's possible. More detrimental to our church has been our pastors' inability to lead the body of Christ in a time of mainline disestablishment when Christians have begun to feel like missionaries in the culture we once thought we owned.

Leading and Preaching in a Divergent Age

It's tough to teach either leadership or preaching in seminary because both of these pastoral tasks are highly contextual. Pastors are wise to be suspicious of quick-fix leadership books with their allegedly knock-down, surefire leadership principles; good leadership is context-dependent. Equally wise to avoid the book titled "How to Preach a Good Sermon Every Sunday."

Before anyone can ask, "Which way ought we to go?" there must be a prior contextual question: "Where are we on the map?"

The chief challenge in my four decades of ministry has been the radical change of cultural context in which we lead and preach. The "good" preaching that once gathered a crowd now ricochets back at the preacher from empty pews in a decade-long "attendance recession," and the good-enough leadership that once maintained a healthy congregation is no longer appropriate for a church that must change or die.

Preachers look out on a conglomeration of people who hardly know one another, making our pious references to our "church community" and our "church family" sound hollow. We boast of diversity and inclusion, but the median age in my denomination is well over sixty. We bishops devised the slogan "Making disciples for the transformation of the world." The gap between our public aspirations and the reality of our results is laughable. There's an embarrassing (bordering on deceitful) disjunction between our grand declarations and our weakened internal condition.

"We're discovering that being a welcoming church requires more than simply unfurling a rainbow flag from our steeple," a pastor said recently. "A series of sermons on why we ought to be an inclusive and welcoming congregation does not a welcoming congregation make." People don't do right by being told in sermons to do right.

Although my church brags of being "inclusive" and "diverse," we have a lower percentage of African American Methodists than we did at the time of my ordination in 1974. We've attempted to substitute slogans and false advertising for the hard, adaptive work of coming to terms with our true condition.

It's not that our past preaching and leadership were wrong; it's just that the changing reality of the church requires that we must work differently. In 2005, I assembled *Sermons from Duke Chapel*, with selections of sermons from the chapel's seventy-five-year history.[1] The same year the book appeared, I became bishop in Alabama. A few months into my episcopacy I realized that none of the sermons I heard preached in the churches I visited sounded like the sermons in the book. In just a couple of decades, the preaching of the gospel had radically changed into direct, personal, energetic, engaged sermons that promised immediate relevance to the listener's situation. None of the hundreds of books on preaching published in the past decade could have been published just a decade before.

Having dramatically changed our preaching, now we must adapt our leadership in light of our new context. Our changed situation is a God-given moment for us pastors to step back and ask not only, "What's the right way to lead?" but also a more basic question: "Which way should we be going here and now?"

What are the chief aspects of our changed context that church leaders ought to note? Gil Rendle, author of *Quietly Courageous*, the decade's most helpful book on church leadership,[2] says that most of us who lead the church today grew up in a *convergent culture*, whereas we now find ourselves leading in a *divergent culture.* A convergent culture is characterized by commonality, a sense of unity, common purpose, and shared values; a divergent culture craves variety and diversity and stresses generational, racial, and gender differences. Whereas a convergent culture urges individuals to hide their differences or to try to fold their differences into the larger group, a divergent culture encourages people to lead with their differences and to cultivate and express the ways they deviate from cultural norms.

Mainline churches like mine thrived in a convergent culture. As Gil says, "It isn't difficult to lead people in the direction they are already going." The questions and the answers are the same for everybody. We dream the same dream. Everybody wants to look average.

The cultural context in which we worked really didn't matter much because it simply confirmed who we were as compliant members of the majority culture. Congregational unity wasn't much of a challenge when we could rely upon an already well-formed common identity and purpose. Rather than creating and inculcating a common, distinctive sense of mission, church leaders could rely on people's desire to fit into the larger group.

At some point people stopped saying, "We're here because my family has always been Baptist" (convergent), and started asking, "What can your church do for us?" (divergent).

Divergent leadership is complex because our organizations and institutions have become multifaceted in ways that are often experienced as fragmented and dissonant. Gil says that a question like "Where is the nearest Presbyterian church?" (convergent) has become "Why do you want to go to a Presbyterian church?" (divergent).

Just as our sermons must appeal to a diverse group of hearers, most of us pastors find ourselves in institutions where we must both attend to the current demands of the congregation and at the same time move our people to a new paradigm. We must continue to know how to do the basic tasks of ministry, to fulfill many of the congregation's traditional expectations, and at the same time constantly be learning how to do what we do not know how to do. Learning and adaptation, experimentation, and discovery are the order of the day. We've got to move from fixation with fixing toward being obsessed with learning, from planning and goal setting to understanding and re-visioning, from asking how to wondering why.

More than one congregation has debated whether or not to begin an additional, alternative worship service different in style and focus from their accustomed service.

"We don't want to split up our congregation between the 'contemporary' and the 'traditional' crowd," some argued.

Most of these churches came to the realization that they were already divided; the new additional service reached those whose worship needs had been denied.

"The easiest, surest way to increase your Sunday attendance," advised one consultant, "is to begin a new service." But then he turned to the pastors and said, "Don't begin a new service unless you are willing to reinvent your preaching. The sermons you've been preaching at your traditional service have been aimed at a different congregation from the one you'll speak to at the new service and will seem out of place in this new context."

Gil thinks the major change from a convergent to a divergent culture is our society's move from "communal" to "individual." Divergent institutions tend to be a conglomeration of individuals. In a divergent age, advertising and technology encourage us to fulfill our individual needs by exercising individual preference.

"I'm trying to lead a church where half of 'em get their news from Fox and the other half from MSNBC," groused one pastor. "While I'm trying to preach the good news that can bring us together, they're trying to pigeonhole my message into one of these two containers."

The media identifies a plethora of segments and plays to our segmentation. We find ourselves living in the functional equivalent of gated communities in which personal preferences tend to outweigh a sense of common purpose. The subjective feelings of individuals, along with the fulfillment of individual desires, preoccupy a diversion culture.

Throughout my ministry I've preached the Christian necessity of a racially, ethnically inclusive and diverse congregation. Yet I never succeeded in forming a congregation that matched my homiletical exhortation. It's difficult to urge a church to violate its divergent expectations for individual fulfillment with talk of merging and converging those differences in one body.

When divergent Millennials say that they don't want to be part of "organized religion," what they mean is that they don't want to be part of a congregation; congregations are the way that Christians organize. Even more troubling theologically, they may be saying they prefer a disincarnate God, Christ without a body. How do we entice people toward an incarnational faith, an embodied spirituality, when they believe their highest calling is to discover and to express their individuality apart from a group?

Curiously, many of these Millennials are more open to preaching—think: one person standing and delivering in a TED Talk—than they are to congregating. They may download a hip preaching video but resist the hard work of rolling up their sleeves and joining a congregation. In such a climate, perhaps preaching becomes a door, an invitation toward our peculiarly corporate Christian way of being spiritual—the congregation.

We've got our work cut out for us in a divergent age because pastors are ordained by the church to lead the church, to be engaged in essentially communal, group, ecclesial concerns. Elsewhere I've called pastors "community persons." Good pastors are ordained to keep building up the Christian community, keep wondering what it takes for this conglomeration of individuals to become the body of Christ, and keep worrying about who's out and what it would take for them to be in.[3]

To be honest, my biblical interpretation and preaching show that I, too, am a child of a divergent age. One of the greatest weaknesses in many of my moves from the biblical text to the preached sermon is that I neglect the communal, corporate intentions of Scripture. I turn a text that addresses the whole congregation into an existential, subjective matter. That's what happens in a radically individualized ("What's in it for *me*?") culture.

So my sermon on 1 Corinthians 13, Paul's great hymn to love, is transformed from Paul's corporately derived and delivered word to a divided church to an exhortation for individuals to be more loving in their daily interactions or, worse, as instructions for a happier marriage.

Scripture tends to be communally concerned before it is individually so. Why do I so seldom preach from the letters of Paul? The epistles arise from essentially in-house, parochial, congregational concerns—urging the rich and the poor to share with one another in the church, pressing people to lay aside their differences and cease squabbling, advising a younger associate to utilize his God-given authority despite his immaturity, pleading for money to help churches in need. In short, Paul's letters are occupied with just the sort of communal, corporate problems that vex pastors. It may be enough for most Christians to tend their own spiritual gardens without much thought for the spiritual growth of their fellow Christians. But not the pastor. Thus in a divergent age, expect tension between the gospel's essentially convergent concerns and those of an individualized, divergent culture.

In a sermon to a divided congregation, I began by noting that division in churches is nothing new. "By my estimate, at least half of Paul's letters are addressed to divided churches. Would Paul have talked so much about love and unity if his churches were actually of one heart and mind?"

Then I launched into a listing of the diverse gifts I had observed among the people at Northside Church:

> Want somebody to pour oil on troubled waters after an acrimonious council meeting? Call Amanda. She can find some good in every person's point of view—even mine!
>
> On the other hand, if you want to see placid waters troubled, some issue put out on the table that most of us would rather avoid, then you know who is in charge of that! Homer, we all know that's you!
>
> Got some new initiative that needs someone to be the sparkplug that gets it up and running and pushes it forward? John Black is the person God has assigned that task in this church.
>
> Need the floor mopped in the fellowship hall after the pipe broke on Christmas Eve? Now who in the world would undertake such a menial task at that time of the year? You know who—Betty Watson. We couldn't

have celebrated Christ's miraculous birth without Betty's mundane work with mop and bucket.

Lost your job and don't know which way to turn? Fortunately, God has equipped a number of folks to help you through the hard times: Johnson, Matt, and Arthur. Just call them and you'll be helped by their business gifts.

Down on your luck and don't know where you'll get $25 to get the electricity turned back on? Come to our clothes closet and ask for Sammie. She's the one God has appointed to do that.

Alonzo, how many people's cars have you got up and running without charging them a dime? More than you can count, right? Glad they didn't come to me in their time of need. God has given you a gift for auto mechanics that God appears to have no intention of giving me! To say nothing of your open-handed generosity.

God has sent this church all the people we need to obey God's call. The world puts before us a wide range of needs. People are hurting in all kinds of ways. So the one Spirit gives us many gifts and then sets us loose in the world.

Let's encourage one another to use the specific gifts God has given us to help others. Let's honor the diversity of gifts and not put down anybody's gift just because it's not the gift that God has given to you.

I'm going to read you some Scripture. Though it was written by Paul two thousand years ago to a church on the shores of the Mediterranean, I think it was written to you, the people of Northside Church on Summit Drive in Greenville:

"There are different spiritual gifts but the same Spirit; and there are different ministries and the same Lord; and there are different activities but the same God who produces all of them in everyone. A demonstration of the Spirit is given to each person for the common good. A word of wisdom is given by the Spirit to one person, a word of knowledge to another . . . , gifts of healing to another . . . , performance of miracles to another, prophecy to another. . . . All these things are produced by the one and same Spirit who gives what he wants to each person. Christ is just like the human body—a body is a unit and has many parts; and all the parts of the body are one body, even though there are many" (1 Cor 12:4–12).

Leaders of divergent organizations find leadership tough as they attempt to negotiate competing aspirations. Distrust of leaders results. The compromises that a leader seeks in order to foster a semblance of unity are often viewed by competing segments of the organization as a betrayal of trust, a sign that the leader lacks integrity and commitment to the segment's cherished ideals.

Personal choice is elevated as the supreme human virtue. My church is good because I chose it, though I retain the option to choose another if my church fails to align itself with my expectations. All institutions become voluntary; individuals view their membership in the organization as their personal choice, and they voluntarily stay with the organization as long as it satisfies their personal preferences. My desire becomes inflated to the level of need, and need quickly elevates to the level of my rights, and because my desires are infinite, I never feel that my right to fulfillment has been satisfied. Woe be unto the pastor who sets out to "serve the needs of my people."

The culture tells us that democracy exists to give each of us the right to have our personal preferences expressed and to have our needs met, as long as we do not interfere with the right of other people to do the same. Tasks like nurturing the common good and building institutions that last and continue to serve the common good are less important than receiving immediate personal satisfaction from our present institutions.

As one pastor put it, "I'm always on probation. People let me know, up front, that they are glad to be members of this church until I fail to preach 'God's word' (as they define it), and then they'll take a walk."

Gil Rendle candidly admits that churches are in a tough situation in a divergent culture because the gospel compels churches to ask more of their members than the contemporary social contract allows. Sustained, active, costly engagement with religious congregations is therefore shrinking. If a person hears our sermons just once a month, that person is now considered a "regular attender." It's too much for leaders to aim for agreement and consensus in a divergent culture. People don't want to move toward the mean, to blend into the average; they want to stand out in their ability to satisfy their own preferences.

A couple of families complained, "Our church doesn't have an active youth group."

"Thank you for honestly noting that," I responded. "Help me to learn how to form a vibrant youth ministry," I pled. "Let's work together to make the best youth ministry in town."

A week later these families left, seeking a church that didn't need them.

The old convergent world stressed uniformity and agreement, discovering and then enforcing the will of the majority. The will of the group superseded the desires of the individual, and the individual was expected to change to fit the group. Majority vote decided everything, and the minority was expected to bow to the will of the majority. The leader was expected to be attentive to what nine out of ten people desired and to encourage the unhappy 10 percent to adjust to the majority's norm.

Muddling Through

In a divergent time, leaders cannot waste energy attempting to foster unity and uniformity; rather, the leader aspires to have the congregation muddle through with enough people on board and a good-enough, workable consensus. Gil Rendle says that consensus is not everybody in agreement, but rather everybody realizing that all the voices have been heard and all agreeing to muddle forward, in spite of continuing disagreements.

After a disastrous special General Conference of the United Methodist Church (UMC), I preached a Lenten sermon on Mark 8:31–33, in which Jesus baffles and shocks his disciples by predicting his death. When Peter expresses his confusion, Jesus rebukes him. Jesus doesn't elaborate; rather, he keeps walking and talking and the disciples keep walking and listening. The disciples don't understand; they have no consensus among themselves, no clue what's going to happen to them in the future. They just keep muddling through with Jesus, which was the title of my sermon.

> What's going to happen to our church after this General Conference vote? I don't know. I expect there will be

schism, posturing by this group or that. Some will leave hurt and angry; some will stay, though they will be miserable and make everyone else so, which is sad.

But the amazing thing is that, even though you don't know the future for our church, and you don't know what comes next, here you have come to worship again this Sunday. In that, you are like Jesus's first disciples. They couldn't understand his talk about the trials ahead. A crucified Messiah? It's unthinkable.

So they just kept listening, just kept talking and arguing, just kept walking with him. And so have you.

Thus my proposal for you this Sunday: Let's muddle through together, with Jesus.

As we muddle on, I promise you: No vote will be taken here that intends finally to silence dissident voices. I plead with everyone to keep talking—more importantly, to keep listening and learning. We will not decide anything once-and-for-all; we'll keep walking with Jesus and expect him to keep working with us. We'll keep checking in with each other, keep evaluating, willing to ditch plans on the basis of what we will learn tomorrow, praying for openness to the leading of the Holy Spirit. We won't expect everyone to agree in order to move forward, but rather that we all agree to muddle on, even with our differences. We won't spend time attempting to control, constrain, or coerce any of you into abandoning your positions, but rather we all agree to be on the way toward possibly different positions. And through it all, we agree to continue to break bread together at the Lord's table.

Now, let's refocus on the most important thing that Jesus asks of us. Let's accept Jesus's invitation to join with one another at his table, invited not because we hold the correct or consensus position on some issue, but rather invited because he loves us all, even in our differences.

Come.

Then, on the Fifth Sunday in Lent of the same year the assigned gospel is John 12:1–8. Word had reached us that some United Methodist churches were threatening to take their expensive church property and bolt from the denomination. After narrating Mary's anointing of Jesus's feet with "expensive perfume," Judas ("one of his disciples") makes a perfectly valid objection that this much money should be "given to the poor," whom Jesus loves. Jesus responds, "Leave her alone," predicting, "You will always have the poor among you, but you won't always have me."

I concluded my sermon that Sunday with the following:

Our church is in a mess, and maybe always has been. With Jesus, sometimes it's not crystal-clear what faith-fulness is supposed to be. We build this costly building to worship a Savior who loves the poor. Jesus's closest disciples are also his most heinous betrayers. The one who raises the dead is on his way to die on a cross. Was Mary right in her extravagant devotion to Christ, or was Judas right in his objection to her act and his advocacy for the poor?

I don't know. Perhaps John tells this story with delib-erate ambiguity because maybe that's the way it is with discipleship—when it comes to faithful discipleship, we just don't know for sure. If Jesus Christ, the soon-to-be-crucified Messiah, is also the Light of the World, there will be gaps in our understanding, disagreements among us about just which way is the path that Jesus wants us to walk.

What are we to do along the way with Jesus? Maybe the best we can do is what I suggested a few Sundays ago: muddle through, keep walking, keep talking, keep listening and learning from one another and from Jesus. Even after we get to the cross and the empty tomb, we'll have more questions, there will be ambiguity—especially there.

Let's muddle through in the faith that at the end of our Lenten journey, we'll get something better than clarity and answers; we'll get Jesus, who stands there to say, "All you muddlers who don't always do right, or know right, I love you, still."

Anxiety amid Complexity

In our divergent age, technology speeds up everything, so we live in a less solid, conceivable, and controllable world. Institutions don't retain their shape for long. Workable patterns of behavior don't last. Our institutions become more amoeba-like. When I took a homiletics course in seminary, we studied "sermon construction," a step-by-step process whereby the preacher logically moved from a biblical text to a well-formed sermon. Today, that process is much more malleable and organic. Sermons need not always be outlined as A to B to C but can be C to A to B and back to C. Definitive, once-and-for-all declarations are less believable than ad hoc hunches about where we seem to be at the moment.

Contemporary preachers rarely aim to construct a solid, stable sermon, but rather strive to produce a sermon that flows, that takes people on a journey of discovery, that fosters space for people to hear the promptings of the Holy Spirit.

Once organizational change moved in a linear fashion. We did a SWOT analysis of the Strengths, Weaknesses, Opportunities, and Threats that we faced. We gathered information, defined the problem, then devised a long-term plan. We applied strategies based on the reasoning "Since this is the fix we're in, what do we do to get out of it?" We set goals and followed timetables. American Progressivism led us to assume that the future could be shaped in orderly, progressive stages. Good leadership was seen as the fruit of logical thinking and analysis that assumed, "This always worked for us in the past; surely it will work again."

The days of linear thinking, applied to solvable problems, are over. We're in a condition whose complexity demands ad hoc, liquid, adaptive response, and good old muddling through.

As the losses mount up for many Americans, their grief and pain propel them to look for some enemy to blame and a savior who will get them back to the good old days.

(That sentence was written in the Atlanta airport as I sat across from a young woman who appeared to be in her teens, wearing a "Make America Great Again" T-shirt.)

I remember hearing the Swedish economist Gunnar Myrdal once say, "There is no such thing as economic problems; there are only problems." Reality is complicated—more complicated than we have the intellectual courage to admit. Much of our thinking, analysis, and rumination is intimidated by the complexity of reality; therefore, oversimplification and reductionism plague modern thought—including this paragraph! There is no clear sense of where we are on the map, no consensus that a map even exists. Because of divergent fragmentation, leaders must cope with a sometimes dizzying array of component parts. Few congregations are composed of only one congregation. Things change quickly, and the change is less predictable than it used to be. Sometimes the leader is the last one to know that things have changed. Although the church may be perceived by many as the one stable presence in the community, when the surrounding context changes radically, the church must learn to adapt to circumstances beyond its control.

Pastor and church consultant Peter Steinke explains that anxiety in a system is compounded whenever the leader lacks a clear vision. "Where there is an unclear vision, the people perish in their own anxious reactivity." Steinke adds, "By articulating a sense of where a group is going, the leader gives it direction and destiny."

Steinke warns that "the vision that defines the group must be forged and safeguarded by leaders who are themselves well-differentiated." The leader must be able to step outside of the leader's self and outside of the exclusively internal concerns of the congregation as the well-differentiated lead missionary who cultivates an unwavering focus on the mission.[4]

In the face of complexity, Gil Rendle says, it's crucial for leaders to know when something is not a *problem*. If a situation does not have a conceivable solution, a specific answer, then it is not a problem; it is a *condition*. A broken bone is a problem that can be fixed by the application of a technical solution. Lung cancer is a complex, baffling, chronic condition that is impervious to simple, technical fixes. Leaders can do harm by attempting to apply technical leadership—that is, tactical, problem-solving leadership—in adaptive, chronic situations that are conditions. Frustration results.

The more anxious a congregation about the changes occurring in its context, the more the congregation will diagnose their church as having a problem and look to us pastoral leaders for clear, simple solutions that promise to reduce their anxiety.

A condition is chronic, requiring everybody creatively to adapt and to become learners. My UMC thought it had a problem that could be solved by majority vote at a General Conference when in reality it has a condition that requires creative adaptation and muddling through. By treating our condition as a problem, we made matters worse.

Most changes that a leader needs to orchestrate require prior change in the soul of the leader. When attempting to lead change, to courageously help a congregation face its true condition, sometimes leaders find they are unable to create or control change; about the best we can do is to manage ourselves as we careen through the change that happens around us. If pastors are reluctant to reinvent themselves as leaders, to learn new skills and ways of relating to their flocks, the most anxious person in the congregation will be the pastor.

Disruptive Leadership

Transformative, change-oriented leadership cannot be accomplished without disrupting and disturbing the homeostasis of the organization. There can be no disruption of the institutional status quo for the repurposing of the organization without the threat of destruction of the security and placid relationships among church members. Some of the relationships between pastor and people are built upon codependency, mutual self-deception, or attachment to inadequate (and even unfaithful) ideas about the church and its ministry. As a pastor I tacitly promise not to question your discipleship or to hold you accountable in exchange for your agreement never to question my pastoral performance. Let's call the resulting charade "church."

While pastoral leaders can't force or control change, we can disturb, push, and disrupt the church so problems are faced and so pain is acknowledged and endured, whereby the congregation is given the possibility of forward movement arising from within the church. Churches cannot remain static—they either grow or they die. Death comes in an organization that is in love with equilibrium and contentment and is too enamored of its history. By asking the right questions, a leader can appropriately disturb an organization rather than grabbing satisfying answers that produce a false sense of calm.

Jesus sometimes brings peace, sometimes a sword. He was a notorious troublemaker, particularly when he preached (Luke 4), because there's no way for God to be with us and to call us without troubling our false gods and assorted deceits and conceits.

It may take time for members of the congregation to learn to expect a sermon to disrupt and dislodge their received ideas. Nearly every biblical passage (interesting: we call a text a "passage"—that is, a path from here to somewhere else) bears with it an implied demand: you will probably have to change in order for this text to make sense.

The preaching of Jesus typifies the disruptive intent of Scripture. Jesus's parables are known for their surprise endings, unexpected twists and turns, and unlikely heroes. Clearly, the parables intend to provoke and to tease us into new ways of thinking and acting, rather than to confirm what we already know.

To help me in my work as bishop in Alabama, I had a framed, faded copy of "Letter from a Birmingham Jail," mimeographed for "Bombingham" clergy a few days after it was issued by King to a group of powerful white clergy like me. In his appeal, Martin Luther King Jr. justifies his marches and sit-ins that "disturbed the peace":

> "Why sit-ins, marches and so forth? Isn't negotiation a better path?" You are quite right in calling for negotiation. . . . Nonviolent direct action seeks to create such a crisis and foster such a tension that a community which has constantly refused to negotiate is forced to confront the issue. It seeks so to dramatize the issue that it can no longer be ignored.[5]

King explains that while he opposes violent tension, he believes there is "a type of constructive, nonviolent tension that is necessary for growth":

> So must we see the need for nonviolent gadflies to create the kind of tension in society that will help men rise from the dark depths of prejudice and racism to the majestic heights of understanding and brotherhood.[6]

The purpose of protests is "to create a situation so crisis-packed that it will inevitably open the door to negotiation."[7] The liberal recipients of King's letter (one of whom was a Methodist bishop) hoped that Birmingham would desegregate without a fight. King eloquently told them they were wrong.[8]

Little good that Jesus wants to do in the world gets done without a preacher like Martin Luther King Jr. who is willing to induce tension.

Mission

These days, few people are interested in joining a church to keep the machinery going or the roof repaired. A new generation of activists don't want to be *supportive* of mission; they want face-to-face, self-involved opportunities to *do* mission. God has made us longing for lives caught up in something greater than ourselves.

Even if people join a church expecting to be served rather than to serve, they must eventually come to terms with Jesus Christ, who is the embodiment of the mission of God and links our salvation to his vocation. We cannot worship Jesus without being with Jesus, doing what he does, going where he goes.

Mission begins with Christ's commissioning. We follow Christ because we have been summoned by Christ. Therefore, vocative preaching is an essential part of mission. We preachers ought to strive, in every sermon, to have some illustration or example whereby ordinary Christian people sense God's vocation. Mission begins in the heart of God, in God's determination to love the world through a missional people. Individual Christians become missionaries when they hear their names called, and a primary way God calls people is through preaching.

One of the greatest hindrances for mission is lack of imagination. Too many people in the church think of mission as something exotic, an event that goes on somewhere else, work other than here through people other than us. In preaching, particularly when stories of mission activity and success are narrated, people are disarmed; they come to see themselves as part of God's gracious activity in the world. I know of no congregation where there is active, bold, engaging mission without vibrant preaching by the pastor, the lead missionary of the missional congregation.

Sometimes pastors are stretched between the God-given purposefulness of the church and the pervasive internal relationality of the congregation. Let's be honest: We want to maintain personal relationships with congregation members, not only because they may be valuable to the congregation, but also because the role of pastor as maintainer and manager of relationships is easier than the role of pastor as mission motivator and equipper.

Sometimes the purposefulness of Scripture and the missional demands placed upon the church by God are the source of the greatest tension in the congregation. God has called us not only to be in relationship with one another but also for the more demanding purpose of joining in God's mission to God's world. To attempt to lessen this vocational tension—this stress that arises from the disjunction between what God calls us to do and how we have contented ourselves with being another loving, caring voluntary association—is to risk reducing the body of Christ to no more than a club of like-minded people.

This tension, this pressure that Jesus applies to his people, can be utilized by pastoral leaders. It's the same tension that is experienced every Sunday in the preparation and delivery of a sermon—the disruptive but potentially life-giving friction between the demands of God's word and the wishes for peace and comfort among God's less-than-faithful people.

The body of Christ atrophies as a parochial, static body in residence, preoccupied with self-care. Resisting the ever-present clerical temptation to be caregivers and managers of an institution, we preachers are called to be "mission movers."[9] We no longer go out to do mission work elsewhere or educate for church membership in a pleasantly Christian America; we call and equip people to be missionaries in a pagan North American mission field. Laity are called not to keep up the church but to be part of the mission of Jesus Christ in the world. The future for the church in our context is in recovering its core—a countercultural, communal, missionary movement empowered by the Holy Spirit that enables people, in service to Jesus Christ, to resist the wiles of the world.

Our great task is not to stabilize, standardize, or harmonize the people of God, but rather to be the church in motion. Jesus Christ is God on the move, and the structures of a congregation should be the bare organizational essentials that are required to keep disciples moving. Sending people out as missionaries precedes bringing people in as members. Social justice and evangelism are the same movement: Jesus's "come unto me" is linked to Jesus's "go into all the world." Today it is more important to experience agitation by the wild, untamed, uncontained power of the Holy Spirit than to submit to control by denominational rules and structures. Enjoyment of the liveliness of the risen Christ is more important than enforcement of uniform ways of being the church.

The characterization of the pastor as leader of missionaries has had invigorating consequences for thought on pastoral leadership. Paul Borden contrasts the pastor as leader of a *maintenance congregation* with the pastor as the igniter of a *mission congregation*:[10]

> When faced with the need for change, the maintenance congregation says, "If this upsets many of our members, we won't do it." The mission congregation says, "If this will help us reach someone outside our congregation, let's take the risk!"
>
> When contemplating congregational innovation, members of the maintenance congregation wonder, "How will this change affect me and my family?" The mission-oriented congregation asks, "Will this change be well received by someone outside my family?"

The maintenance congregation says, "The main thing is to be faithful to our past." The mission congregation says, "The main thing is to be faithful to God's promised future." With a resurrected Christ, we have more future ahead of us than past behind us.

The pastor of a maintenance congregation says to a newcomer, "Let me introduce you to some of our members whom you will like." The mission pastor says to prospective and new members, "Here's how you can help us be a more faithful congregation. How can we help you be more faithful to your vocation?"

When confronted with some legitimate pastoral concern, the maintenance pastor asks, "How can I meet this need?" The missional congregation pastor asks, "How can this need be met?" The chief caregiver within the congregation is the congregation, not the pastor; the main missionary is the whole people of God.

The maintenance congregation asks, "How many Methodists live in our area?" The missional congregation asks, "How many unchurched people live within twenty minutes of this church?"

"How can we get these people to support our church?" asks the maintenance congregation. The mission congregation asks, "What can we do to support these people?"

The maintenance congregation wonders, "How can we save this congregation?" The mission congregation asks, "How can we participate in God's salvation of the world?"

Borden says that, avoiding conflict at any cost, the maintenance congregation usually succeeds only at suppressing conflict by focusing upon trivialities. The mission congregation understands that conflict comes with obedience to the mission of Jesus Christ. Our main task is not the avoidance of pain, or the quelling of all disagreement and conflict; our task is to participate in the mission of Christ and to engage the conflict that comes with the gospel's interaction with the world rather than bog down in internal congregational squabbling.

"Bishop," the lay leader said to me, "Carl is a wonderfully attentive, loving, and caring pastor."

"Glad to hear that," I said.

"But the numbers indicate that our church is going out of business. Carl is loving our church into the grave. Our next pastor has got to be better than a loving pastor. The next guy has got to have the guts to lead."

As bishop I inherited a mission statement for my conference: *Every church challenged and equipped to make disciples for Jesus Christ by taking risks and changing lives.* That statement wonderfully empowered my leadership. I would routinely begin meetings with recitation of that statement. I would end meetings of the bishop's cabinet by asking, "Name two or three risks we have taken during this meeting." When I visited churches, I would always try to work in the question "What's one risk you have taken in the past year that might enable you to be the body of Christ in motion?"

One reason our role as pastor is subordinate to our role as preacher is that risk is a characteristic of engaging preaching. As Karl Barth said, "Preachers dare."[11] In sermons we risk intruding into people's settled arrangements with God, daring to offer new ways of construing their lives, hazarding talk about subjects they have been avoiding.

Like preaching, leadership is a performance. Every day a pastor is forced by the needs of the church and the call of God to act like a spiritual leader even when the pastor doesn't feel like it, even when, by want of character or inclination, the pastor is personally not well suited to the demands of the role. Someone must subordinate personal feelings and reservations and go ahead and lead, or the congregation founders in indecision and lack of direction. When there is a leadership vacuum, with no one accepting responsibility to lead, other power brokers usually step up and compound the corporate misery.

Peter Gomes, Harvard's late, great preacher, often said to me, "Interesting sermons take risks." To take a congregation deeper than they expected, to venture beyond common sense, to hazard encounter with a living God without our self-protective intellectual armor is to be on our way to more engaging preaching.

When the congregation asks, "Is there any word from the Lord?" and we merely human beings stand up and preach, that's risky. They erroneously think they have authorized you to be the always loving, caring, patient, and inoffensive pastor. By God's grace you might dare to be even more: the courageous leader. Good preachers always venture saying more than the congregation wanted said.

To pray an epiclesis, a prayer for the Holy Spirit, just before a sermon is risky business. In the power of the Holy Spirit, our words may become God's summons, the beginning of God-induced disruption, church on the way to adventure.

Congregations bestow authority upon their preachers to speak, but not to speak beyond the point of discomfort. The congregation longs for a preacher who reduces their intellectual anxiety and leads them back to a safe sense of comfortable equilibrium. When that doesn't happen, sometimes they will work to sabotage and discredit the preacher. So, Gil Rendle says, if the preacher really wants to move a congregation forward by provoking change, the preacher must dare to exceed the level of authority that the people willingly give.[12]

I remember Walter Brueggemann telling us preachers, "If you are a coward by nature, God can still use you. You can get down behind the biblical text and push that out toward the congregation, peeking out from behind the text and saying, 'I'm not necessarily saying this, but I do think the text does.'"

In service to the leadership needs of our congregations, we preachers must find a way to love the Lord who speaks from the biblical text more than we love our people, or more properly, we must love our people in the same way that Jesus loves them—as his missionaries, Christ's answer to what's wrong with the world.

Priorities

As bishop, I determined never to appoint a pastor I had not heard preach. Pastors submitted recordings of two of their sermons during the appointive process. Listening to my preachers' sermons, I learned that one of a preacher's greatest challenges is clarity. The laity complain that their preachers tackle too many subjects, wander down too many divergent paths, and are therefore difficult to follow.

Many sermons lack clarity because preachers have failed to prioritize what they most want to say in the sermon. Too many ideas are taken on, and listeners are frustrated because the sermon moves in too many competing directions. I therefore still find helpful the time-honored practice of writing down the theme of the sermon in one sentence and allowing that sentence to govern the subject and flow of the sermon. The truth of Jesus Christ is so complex and multivalent, and biblical texts so thick and layered with meaning, that prioritizing is a major task of sermon preparation.

If prioritizing the ideas and intentions of a sermon is a challenge for us as preachers, it's also a challenge for us as pastoral leaders. Healthy congregations have clarity about their corporate identity and can clearly communicate that identity to others. While vibrant congregations tend to be diverse in the individual identities of their members and to draw on diverse sources for their vibrancy, they share an ability to clearly name who God means them to be and who they are not meant to be.

Any organization that takes upon itself the mission of being Christ's visible, active presence in the world—going into all the world in his name, telling and showing the good news to all—had better be good at prioritizing. What do we most need to do at this point in time? Left to their own devices, churches do what they have been doing. If they have always had a paid staff member to lead youth ministry, then they will fight to retain that paid staff member without evaluating the suitability of this ministry in vastly changed circumstances.

A priority is that to which we give attention and for which we accept responsibility. Sometimes the greatest challenge in setting a priority is in making painful decisions about what we will no longer do. The easiest thing is simply to add more priorities onto the work we've been doing. The business of the church becomes busyness. Fatigue sets in.

I heard Henri Nouwen declare to pastors that if you don't know the absolutely essential, you'll do the merely important, and since so much that pastors do is important, no wonder pastors are often resentful of those they so busily serve.

Sometimes a plethora of priorities is a sign of functional atheism at work—unless we undertake specific work, the work won't get done. Setting priorities requires appropriate humility that admits that while some work is important, it is not work that God has entrusted to *us*. God will have to undertake this ministry through another congregation. Sometimes pastoral fatigue or congregational financial stress is an indicator that a congregation has not done the courageous work of specifying what they will no longer do. The courageous leader helps the congregation say that some work is more important than other work *for this congregation.*

Purpose

Before asking what we should do, adaptive leadership poses questions of *identity* (Who are we?), of *purpose* (Why are we here?), and of *goals* (Where are we being called to go?). I felt judged and convicted by Ron Heifetz's counsel to do sufficient reflection, discussion, and assessment and thereby "resist the leap into action."[13] The adaptive leader patiently leads the organization in spending time interpreting and evaluating the body's purpose.[14] In my own leadership, my desire to appear to be a decisive leader sometimes tempted me to rush decisions and address issues before they had time to ripen. The result was sometimes a lonely leader who looked behind myself and saw few followers.

Because the mission of the church—the church's reason for being—is both countercultural and counter to our natural dispositions, it must constantly be refurbished. The church is here because God wills it. Whatever God wants to accomplish, God has chosen not to do it alone. That's why for some time it has been said that the church doesn't *have* a mission: the church *is* mission. The church happens when God's people join in *God's* mission, for God's salvation of God's world. From the beginning of the Christian movement, as far back as the Way in Acts, mission has been impossible without mission leaders.

The Lutheran *Augsburg Confession* (1530) defines the church as "the congregation of the saints in which the gospel is rightly preached and the sacraments are rightly administered." While the Reformers' stress upon the church as "congregation" (all the people of God are the "saints") and the emphasis upon preaching and sacraments at the center of the church's life are noteworthy, there is no mention of mission. Against the Protestant Reformers I contend that preaching is not the purpose of the church and its ministry; preaching is a necessary act of mission leadership on the way to mission.

The great enemy of mission, in countless congregations, is the temptation to reduce the church to a conclave of friendly folks who exist for themselves rather than as agents of God's mission to God's world. Internal relationships take priority over missional purpose. Therefore, we Christian leaders must discipline ourselves to remain accountable to those disciplines that take the church outside itself.

In *Good to Great*, Jim Collins puts forth "the Hedgehog Concept," which involves "passion (understanding what your organization stands for and why it exists), best at (understanding what your organization uniquely contributes better than anyone else), and resources (what capacities does your organization have for making its contributions to the world)."[15]

Some of the most important leadership that occurs through preaching involves articulation of and reiteration of the purpose of the congregation. Change begins and is sustained only when there is constant refurbishment of core purpose. It is not enough to assert even our cherished beliefs. The courageous questions that sermons answer are: Why are we here? To whom are we accountable? What is the work that God has given us to do? What good work will we not undertake but allow other churches to handle? What is the shape and purpose of the unique witness to which this congregation is called?

Appreciative inquiry into our strengths can move us from a posture of scarcity—we lack the people, the resources, and the time to do all that we ought to be doing—to a receptivity to the grace that is already present in the congregation, moving from lament over all our failings to celebration of abundance. Basic questions are: What are we good at? Which members of our congregation are God's greatest gifts in the accomplishment of God's mission? What is our "on-ramp"— that is, where have we already succeeded and how can we improve that ministry?

A pastor gave me this testimonial of how she helped a congregation discover its strengths for ministry through a sermon:

> I complained to myself and my husband that I feared that our congregation was aging out of ministry. Our median age was rising. Our largest demographic was older women, most of whom were widows. And then, prodded by the Holy Spirit, my eyes opened to see the numbers of latchkey children in our neighborhood, coming home from school in the afternoon to empty homes. So, I preached a sermon on how God called the child, Samuel (1 Samuel 3), waking the little boy in the night with "Samuel, Samuel . . ."

I asked, "Isn't it amazing that God came so dramatically to the little boy and not to the aging, theologically trained priest, Eli? And yet (please note this carefully, folks), even though God called little Samuel by name, there was still something for Eli to do for the child. Eli had to tell the confused little boy, 'Next time, when you hear your name called, say, "Master, speak, thy servant heareth."

"The little boy didn't yet know enough about God to know that the voice in the night was God's. Eli had to help him discern, had to teach him about God before the boy could know how to respond."

I then recalled how much I owe to my grandmother who kept me after school each day until my mom came home. "I bet some of you have had similar experiences of being guided by an older adult. I'm sure some of you are Christians today because some older person, maybe a relative, often not, helped you know that God was calling you."

I gave some statistics on the plight of children and families in our town and the growing number of working, single-parent homes. Then I said, "This church lacks lots of things that many other congregations enjoy. But one thing we've got is a surplus of grandparents. This room is full of wisdom this morning. I'm looking out upon people with years of experience in parenting and grandparenting. You may be God's gift to some struggling single parent who is trying to be a good parent [all] alone. You could be just the person to show a child that she's loved and cherished by someone outside her home. Maybe you are the person God has designated to tell and to show a child that God loves him and has plans for him. Does anybody here this morning want to play old Eli to young Samuel and help God find a new way to call a new generation?"

That was the beginning of our church's after-school ministry. Refreshments, help with homework, Bible study, the works. Turns out, those children have parents. That means that our congregation is at last growing! I've now got a bunch of older adults who've got something worthwhile to do with their golden years.

It all began with a sermon.

Churches are often characterized by exaggerated aspirations and unrealistic expectations for themselves. They must move from good intentions toward specific expectations and measurable outcomes. Dishonesty about results can lead us to exaggerated, atheistic delusions about our potency or to atheistic despair over our incapacity.

In focusing on what we're doing well, the pastor becomes a steward of the God-given potential within the congregation, rather than the dour critic who, Sunday after Sunday, points out the deficiencies within the organization. The preacher is cast into the role of a fellow learner, one who is surprised that, despite everything, God is at work among ordinary people to accomplish God's extraordinary purposes. The work that we do is God's work, in God's world, to accomplish God's mission, before it is ours.

While both a sense of purpose and good relationships are required for effective pastoral leadership, it is dangerous to the health of a church to make relationship a priority and to fear the dissolution of relationships more than we fear infidelity to our

God-given purpose. It's easier to try to be friendly than faithful, polite rather than productive.

When an offended or hurt individual or family withdraws because of damaged relationality, it's a rare pastor who will risk a conversation about why they've left; it's too painful. Therefore, congregations get by with low expectations for relationships. Christian community lapses into simple cordiality. People are allowed to join by stepping over a very low threshold of entrance and are able to exit with little resistance. The purpose of the church and its ministry is degraded into a club mentality, and pressure is increased on the pastor not to rock the boat but keep everybody happy.

Even though personal relationships are an insufficient base for preaching and leadership, pastoral leadership is always exercised in community. A pastor's work is evoked, formed, confirmed, punished, and rewarded by the people the pastor serves. It's important, therefore, for pastors to be clear that their role in interacting with parishioners is differentiated as a pastoral leader and guide, not that of a personal friend.

Learning to Lead

Gil Rendle says that many of us clergy are talented but "tenuous,"[16] lacking the self-differentiation that gives us the confidence to lead. Peter Steinke earlier taught us that the self-defined leader is secure in the role he or she is called to fulfill. Such a leader is thereby better able to focus upon:

self, not others,
strength, not weakness,

process, not content,
challenge, not comfort,
integrity, not unity,
system, not symptom,
direction, not condition.[17]

The role-differentiated leader is less reactive and more thoughtful in responding to potentially threatening leadership situations, being true to oneself but connected to others, clear about to whom he or she is accountable, disciplining the way he or she reacts to the comments or actions of others.

In order to achieve a higher level of self-differentiation, the leader must become a better observer of one's own emotional reactiveness so that rather than reacting instinctively, one can choose how to respond to a particular situation and thereby better manage a congregation's conflict and anxiety.

Preachers are also "God-differentiated," detached enough from the church to be heavily invested in the church *in Jesus's name*. Our vocation differentiates us as those who are accountable to a boss who is greater than the fickle, totalitarian praise or blame of the congregation. It is powerful freedom to know that you are owned, authorized, claimed, named, and sent by God.

A primary way to gain self-confidence is by learning the principles, insights, and skills needed to be quietly courageous leaders of change in the church. Even more important is the constant refurbishment of our sense of vocation. We preach and lead through external authorization. Our call to leadership was God's idea before it was ours.

Why should we be standing up in front of the congregation and speaking to them from the pulpit? God only knows.

Why should I be the one to step up, take responsibility, tell the truth, and wade into the chaos required for change? God only knows.

In learning to preach, there is usually a long period when the novice preacher struggles to "find my voice," learning to trust God's vocation, gaining self-confidence in the homiletical arts, and finding something that's worth saying in the pulpit. Bold-ness in the pulpit is also born from the conviction that Jesus Christ is indeed the whole truth about God ("We preach not ourselves," 2 Cor 4:5 KJV), that he shall reign, and that he has authorized us, even us, to lead from the pulpit.

For most of us, seminary wasn't much help in teaching us how to lead. Seminaries are better places to learn the classical disciplines of ministry—the riches of the church's orthodox faith, the essential basics for preaching and proclamation—and less helpful in instilling self-confidence for leadership. As Gil Rendle notes, at their best, seminaries offer seminarians infor-mation, skills, and insights rather than helping future pastors to be quietly courageous.[18] The best the seminary can strive for is to produce graduates who are self-confident in their ability to continually learn the leadership qualities that the academy is unable to teach.

The optimum context for learning the courage to speak the truth is not seminary but in a small, trusting, and trustwor-thy intentional peer group who covenants to grow together as preachers. A key to such groups functioning well is that they are made up of those who have the greatest capacities to grow and sufficient courage to submit to the oversight of their peers.

The Sunday after the horror of the Charleston massacre, in a sermon on David's defeat of the giant Goliath, Abby Kocher courageously encouraged the parents in her North Carolina congregation to find a way to talk with their children like Christians about the giant sin of racism. Abby preaches as a pastor, as a parent, and as someone whose parents helped her come to terms with race, not shielding Abby from the truth but rather putting her in a context where she might experience the truth about race:

> As parents, one of the hardest things we have to reckon with is when to protect our children and when to let them encounter the world as it is, in its raw reality, and help them make meaning of what they see. . . . A lot of our focus has been on the long-troubled history about race in this country. . . . But I'm convinced that in addition to . . . deepening our understanding of the past [we must] look forward, . . . interpreting to our younger generations what is unfolding, so that they are prepared, with open eyes. . . .
>
> When I was a child, my parents made a decision that had a profound influence on my life. We lived in eastern North Carolina in a small town . . . in a neighborhood that was changing rapidly. White families were moving out and black families were moving in. . . . Whites were becoming a minority, both in the neighborhood and at school. And my parents decided our family would stay. . . .
>
> My parents did not assume that the more protected I was from racial realities, the stronger I would be. They assumed that learning and strength would come as I encountered the world as it is, and . . . they did so alongside me, and helped me to make meaning of what I saw and heard. They assumed I'd learn more about

race relations on the playground than I could from the newspaper. . . . They let me learn what it meant to be white from the black girls who were fascinated with my hair . . . as we sat around at recess braiding each other's hair, discovering the ways it was different. . . .

I came to understand that I was privileged simply because I was white. . . . My parents didn't protect me from discovering those things. They empowered me to learn. . . .

[Here the preacher recounts the courageous witness of the victims' families at Mother Emanuel African Methodist Episcopal Church after the Charleston massacre.]

To speak such words in faith is to stand as David before Goliath, and to believe that God's power to forgive, God's power to redeem, God's power to bring life out of death is stronger than anything that could be taken away, especially any human ability to take away life.[19]

Faithful pastoral leaders find a way to lead from the pulpit, courageously enabling their congregations to talk about difficult matters, transforming their congregations into free, open space where we demonstrate that Christ gives us the resources to speak truthfully of things the world can't discuss, helping them to restore the adventure to their lives as disciples. Then they accompany their people into the challenging tasks of not only loving Jesus in church but obeying him in the world.

5

Preaching: Telling the Truth about Jesus Christ

The church called it "The Acts of the Apostles" but could have justifiably labeled it "Christian Leadership 101." Acts narrates the history of the earliest churches by telling of the trials, tribulations, and triumphs of the church's first leaders, along with people's response to their leadership and sermons. Acts is known for its many well-crafted, succinct sermons by preachers like Paul and Peter. When a group is under orders from the Holy Spirit, answerable to a truth so odd and countercultural as the gospel of Jesus Christ, its leaders will need that peculiar truth to be reiterated along the way.

> A man named Ananias, along with his wife Sapphira, sold a piece of property. With his wife's knowledge, he withheld some of the proceeds from the sale. He brought the rest and placed it in the care and under the authority of the apostles. Peter asked, "Ananias, how is it that Satan has influenced you to lie to the Holy Spirit by

withholding some of the proceeds from the sale of your land? Wasn't that property yours to keep? . . . You haven't lied to other people but to God!" When Ananias heard these words, he dropped dead. Everyone who heard this conversation was terrified. Some young men stood up, wrapped up his body, carried him out, and buried him.

About three hours later, his wife entered, but she didn't know what had happened to her husband. Peter asked her, "Tell me, did you and your husband receive this price for the field?" She responded, "Yes, that's the amount."

He replied, "How could you scheme with each other to challenge the Lord's Spirit? Look! The feet of those who buried your husband are at the door. They will carry you out too." At that very moment, she dropped dead at his feet. When the young men entered and found her dead, they carried her out and buried her with her husband. Trepidation and dread seized the whole church and all who heard what had happened. (Acts 5:1–11)

It's a peculiar story, and funny. Let's read Acts 5:1–11 as an account of early Christian congregational leadership through courageous truth-telling. Too many church meetings are dull; here's one that became a life-and-death encounter because Peter dared to be a servant leader who told the truth. At first glance, two prominent church members, Ananias and Sapphira, let their greed get away with them. Upon closer inspection, we find that Peter publicly accuses them, not of greed, but of lying to the Holy Spirit (5:3). When Peter introduces God into the conversation, trouble begins. Peter tells them, "You did not lie to us but to God!" (5:4). In Acts, lying to the church is lying to God. Ananias drops dead.

What sort of pastor would provoke so lethal a response to a sermon? Despite their wealth, Ananias and Sapphira are also poor, struggling sinners deserving pastoral empathy rather than rebuke; I'm a more sensitive, caring pastor than Peter.

Truth to tell, I am less wedded to the truth, less willing to confront and to call to account, less willing to insert God into the conversation, particularly if the recipients of my pastoral leadership are a pair of well-heeled laity. Ananias and Sapphira were willing to part with two-thirds of their property. In the churches I've served, that's not called lying; it's spectacular stewardship.

Unlike me, Peter appears to consider truthful leadership superior to what passes for church administration in the churches I've served—protective hand-holding, empathetic paternalism, coddling of parishioners' self-deceit. Peter is committed to the nurturance, not of a loving, caring, community (Rotary or your local bar), but rather of a People of the Truth. Though the truth hurts, lies are the death of community, at least any community that hopes to be a prophetic people of truth in service to the Lord who is the Way, the Life, and the Truth (John 14:6). Perhaps that's why here is Acts' first use of the name "church" (5:11).

Thus we have noted that the adaptive, transformative Christian leader must be the sort of person who summons the resources to tell a congregation the painful truth it has been avoiding. There can be no life-giving change without someone willing to take responsibility, brave the discomfort, and say in the name of Christ, "We need to talk."

To Tell the Truth

Preaching is necessary because the church is constituted upon the conviction that without truthful speech, we cannot sustain the trust necessary to be people who abide in Christ and in one another. Accordingly, preachers are set aside to exercise the authority necessary to sustain the disciplines that make our community peculiarly Christian.

Paul says that preaching the truth in love is one way we foster a congregation's maturation: "Speaking the truth with love, let's grow in every way into Christ" (Eph 4:15), implying that Christians get stuck in their immaturity when a pastor doesn't love the people enough to speak the truth.

I recount the story of Peter, Ananias, and Sapphira in order to accentuate the peculiar nature of leadership in the name of Christ. Christian leadership and proclamation are risky, abrasive, and difficult because they are performed in service to the truth about God (Jesus Christ) rather than in servility to popularity, comfort, stress-reduction, efficiency, productivity, or celebrity. As challenging as witnessing to the truth can be, pity the poor preacher who attempts to base ministry upon a pleasing personality rather than a truthful one.

In preaching, you'll know it's not the gospel if it purports to offer a formula for living with and loving Jesus without discomfort. In the face of all my homiletic attempts to make Jesus more comforting and comfortable, I hear Jesus ask, "What about the word *cross* do you not get?"

In the middle of his commentary on Isaiah the prophet-poet-preacher, Martin Luther exclaims,

> How difficult an occupation preaching is. Indeed, to preach the Word of God is nothing less than to bring

upon oneself all the furies of hell and of Satan, and therefore also of . . . every power of this world. It is the most dangerous kind of life to throw oneself in the way of Satan's many teeth.[1]

Preaching is perilous. Where the word of God is rightly preached, demons are unleashed. Satan does not give up territory without a fight. Because of the demonic resistance to the truth, failure is always possible; the cross looms over the words of even the most faithful preachers.

Still, Christian preaching cannot rest content with speaking the truth; we must lead the congregation in performing the truth. In December of 1955, after Rosa Parks was forced off a bus in Montgomery, Alabama, and arrested, clergy responded by organizing a one-day protest of the city's buses. Black ministers and leaders held a mass meeting at Holt Street Baptist Church to discuss the possibility of extending the boycott into a long-term campaign. Martin Luther King Jr. was a young pastor, new in town. Toward the end of the meeting, one of the leaders asked young preacher King to speak: "We're going to work with grim and bold determination to gain justice on the buses in this city. And we are not wrong. . . . If we are wrong, the Supreme Court of this nation is wrong. If we are wrong, the Constitution of the United States is wrong. If we are wrong, God Almighty is wrong." The night had begun as a meeting; in the course of King's sermon, it became a movement. The word preached led to the word performed.

When he was elected as the boycott group's first president, King preached, "We have no alternative but to protest. For many years we have shown an amazing patience. We have sometimes given our white brothers the feeling that we liked the way we were being treated. But we come here tonight to be saved from

that patience that makes us patient with anything less than freedom and justice."

Shortly thereafter, when King's home was bombed, King
told the angry crowd that gathered, "Be calm as I and my family are. We are not hurt, and remember that if anything happens to me, there will be others to take my place." City officials
obtained injunctions against the boycott in February 1956 and
indicted over eighty boycott leaders, including King, who was
tried and convicted on the charge and ordered to pay $500 or
serve 386 days in jail. National press coverage of the boycott
began, and King said in a TV interview, "It is more honorable
to walk in dignity than ride in humiliation. So . . . we decided
to substitute tired feet for tired souls, and walk the streets of
Montgomery."

King's role in the birth of the Montgomery boycott stands
as an example of the power of skillful rhetoric combined with
shrewd organizational skills, the truth preached calling forth a
movement of truthful people. King's preaching gave ordinary
Christians a vision of themselves as God's agents and reminds us
of what God can do once preaching is linked with courageous
leadership.

Humbly Obedient to the Truth

In preaching classes, I would sometimes chide the student who
spoke too softly, who failed to project voice and gestures into the
congregation. "You've got to find a way to gain self-confidence
in order to win a hearing," I would say.

In some cases, I discovered that their problem was not gospel-
induced humility. It was, rather, a curious pride, an unwillingness to submit to Christ's vocation to preach, a posture that said,

in effect, "Clinging to my preconceptions of how a self-effacing Christian should appear and nurturing my own resistance to serving as your preacher are more important to me than your need to hear the word of God."

Christian leaders are called to Christ-like humility, but it is a humility born of obedience to God and to God's will for the church rather than cowering before a contentious congregation.

After a squabble among the disciples over who is the most prominent in the realm of God, Jesus gives (rare) explicit instruction on leadership:

> You know that those who rule the Gentiles show off their authority over them and their high-ranking officials order them around. But that's not the way it will be with you. Whoever wants to be great among you will be your servant. Whoever wants to be first among you will be your slave—just as the Human One didn't come to be served but rather to serve and to give his life to liberate many people. (Matt 20:25–28)

The way I read it, Jesus is not advocating humility as a general disposition among his disciples, but rather service in the form of the one who "didn't come to be served but rather to serve and to give his life to liberate many." Jesus's peculiar service, we shall soon discover when we arrive at Gethsemane, is born of obedience to the will of the Father. Jesus is humble in his courageous determination to accomplish his redemptive task.

Pompous, self-important, domineering leaders may be the problem in some church families, but not in mine. More typical of us mainline pastors is a tentative, anxious failure of nerve masquerading as humility. Therefore, we pastors must humble ourselves before God's determination to have a faithful witness, a people who testify, in word and deed, in proclamation and mission to the truth about God.

As the great theologian Bob Dylan said, "You've gotta serve somebody." The issue for us leaders is not "Will I be subservient?" but rather "To whom will I be accountable? Whose interests will I serve? To whose truth will I be obedient?"

Timing the Truth

Aristotle taught that truth-telling required prudence. The truth must be told at the right time, for the right reasons, in the right way. Some of my most painful leadership failures were due to my impatience. I was pushing the right truth, for all the right reasons, but at the wrong time. Skilled leadership requires patience with the pace of our followers' tempo of understanding, waiting for the Holy Spirit to stir their imaginations, biding time until the right people catch a glimpse of where we are trying to lead the church so they will then step up and say, "Here am I, send me!"

Truth told too soon in a sermon, without proper preparation, provokes our hearers' defenses that defeat their reception of the truth. Pacing the movement of a sermon through time is usually the last-acquired homiletical skill. Experienced preachers learn how to use silence in a sermon, when to offer the pregnant pause, how to pique their listeners' interest, teasing, building tension, making them wait for resolution of questions and problems that may have been raised earlier in the sermon.

Ron Heifetz, in his discussion of the importance of timing in leadership, uses the example of Lyndon Johnson.[2] Johnson was deeply committed to the passage of a Civil Rights bill. He was sympathetic to Civil Rights leaders' urgings to act decisively in the cause of racial justice and confident that he had the personal political clout to push his party's leaders into passing a bill. But rather than use his power, Johnson waited. He allowed the issue to bubble and boil, waiting until his allies could be identified, giving others the time to step up and help lead the passage of Civil Rights legislation.

Then Martin Luther King was assassinated. Johnson came on national TV and said, "I'm sure you agree, now's the time. Now we must act!" Bipartisan Civil Rights legislation was swift in coming. Johnson got much wider support and better legislation than if he had not disciplined himself to wait until the time was right.

As Lovett Weems explains, "Leadership often requires pacing the work in order to deal with change at a rate people can stand. . . . If the tension is too little, there is no growth; if too great, there is too much anxiety for constructive change."[3]

At what time does a sermon begin? There are sermons that begin back in a pastor's childhood only to await being preached two or three decades later. Some sermons have their birth in an offhand comment by someone during a meeting, a remark that burrows deep in the pastor's consciousness (or sticks in the pastor's craw), to be developed and preached months later.

In a sermon I quoted Karl Barth saying that, when it comes to the Christian faith, we "never lose our amateur status." We never become so adept in the faith that we have no need for God to send us back to the "little league" to learn all over again how to play the game.

A person (a coach!) came out of church and said, "Great quote about our being amateurs. Very helpful. How long did it take you to write that sermon?"

I got that quote during my second year of seminary in my first introduction to Karl Barth.

"How long to prepare?" I replied. "Thirty years."

In one of my early congregations, I proposed following the new Word and Table pattern of worship that was being commended in our denomination, moving the sermon earlier in the service to be followed by the offering, prayers for others, baptisms and communion as responses to the Word.

The worship committee flatly rejected my proposal as too radical and disruptive, using the eight words that strike fear in every leader's heart: "This is the way we've always done it."

Though I wanted to tell them that I knew a lot more about liturgy than they, I didn't. I continued to quietly, unobtrusively push the issue, speaking about how Christian worship is more than singing a hymn, sitting through a sermon, then going home to lunch; truly Christian worship is responsive and responsible, gathering us in worship so that we might be sent forth in mission.

More than a year later I brought up the issue of having the sermon earlier in the Sunday service. Again, there was resistance. So I said, "I really think you will find this new pattern to be a blessing. How about we try a short-term experiment? Let's do it as a trial run over a couple of months, and then I promise we'll have a thorough evaluation. If you still don't like having the sermon earlier in the service, with more acts of worship moved to after the sermon, then I'll gladly talk about it" (never promising that I would revert, only that I would listen to their objections).

They agreed.

I changed the service to the Word and Table pattern and braced myself for their response. I received only positive feedback.

Only two months later, I tell you, when I said, "I promised we would review our practices. Should we move the sermon back to its usual place at the end of the service?" the very person who had led the earlier resistance actually said, "We've always had the sermon early in the service followed by our response to God's word. You have changed so many things about this church, please don't change this."

"Thanks for your feedback," I said, flabbergasted.

6

Pastors as Preachers

Preaching typically occurs when a pastor, who is known, arises in the midst of a congregation of worshippers, who are known, and speaks what is known of the gospel. An anonymous sermon from a stranger who is nowhere in particular, preached to nobody in particular, is less than preaching's contextualization of the gospel is meant to be.

A leader who never articulates a vision to the followers, who has an incoherent message saying little and demanding no response from the hearers, is less than the aspirations of Christian leadership.

Fortunately, the day-to-day responsibilities of pastors provide ideal opportunities for sermon preparation. A major challenge for seminary homiletics classes is that instruction tends to characterize preaching in a detached, theoretical way. Sermons are apt to be seen as a set of ideas that are tossed out to a homiletics professor rather than as what sermons are meant to be—a pastor speaking to a flock in order to lead them in walking the way of Christ.

While sermons are not the only leadership tool at the pastor's disposal, sermons lead when they

* read people into the story of Christ's salvation of the world;
* clarify the purpose and mission of the church;
* recruit and energize people to get behind Jesus's mission in God's world;
* model how to think like Christians;
* motivate and encourage people to draw near to God;
* tell the truth about us and the world through the lens of Scripture.

Exegeting the Context

Try to recycle an old sermon in a different congregation or even in the same congregation a few years later, and you will find that context intrudes powerfully, making a different, and often less appropriate, sermon.

A "good sermon" is preached by someone who has asked, and answered to some degree, basic contextual questions: Who are the hearers? What time is it? Where are we on the map? Who is the God who has convened us? What does God expect of this congregation here, now?

In my first congregation I made a list of characteristics I had learned about the people during my first months as pastor:

They don't read much; the Bible is the only book that helps them find their way; they are fearful of the future because of their economic status (barely getting by from week to week); they haven't had the educational and cultural advantages that I've had; the church is over a hundred years old and they fear they've got more past than future; their church provides them with their main social interaction; they see themselves as sacrificing for their families so that their children will have it easier than they; their racial attitudes are one of the ways that the privileged classes have kept them down; they are suspicious of a seminary-trained preacher; they think I'm too young to be a pastor.

It was helpful for me to exegete my congregation in order to be honest about my limitations as their preacher, the communication challenges before me, and the ways that they believed in the power of preaching more than I.

By the way, my list of congregational characteristics had immediate applications for my leadership. Fresh out of seminary, immersed in graduate school, I had to relearn how to communicate so that my people could understand me. Hearing that my denomination published devotional literature on an eighth-grade reading level, I subscribed to all of their publications. The theology was often less than inspiring, but the ability to communicate was wonderfully formative upon me as a budding preacher.

Tailoring his manner of speech to his strange subject matter, and to his assessments of the Corinthian context, Paul says that he chose a foolish sort of preaching that was congruent with his theological message:

> When I came to you, brothers and sisters, I didn't come preaching God's secrets to you like I was an expert in

speech or wisdom. I had made up my mind not to think about anything while I was with you except Jesus Christ, and to preach him as crucified. I stood in front of you with weakness, fear, and a lot of shaking. My message and my preaching weren't presented with convincing wise words but with a demonstration of the Spirit and of power. I did this so that your faith might not depend on the wisdom of people but on the power of God. (1 Cor 2:1–5)

This is probably our earliest, most explicit statement on the peculiarity of Christian preaching, and one of the few places in the New Testament where a preacher turns aside from the task of proclamation to discuss the homiletical decisions he made on the way to proclamation. Paul the leader adjusts his preaching performance to the particular congregational context to which he is preaching.

In light of his assessment of the Corinthians' triumphalist hyper-spiritualism (I'm assuming that was their main problem), Paul decided to proclaim nothing but "Jesus Christ, and to preach him as crucified." Paul's manner of presentation, his delivery, was "with weakness, fear, and a lot of shaking," a rather peculiar demeanor for a public speaker. Why? So that nothing might move or convince his hearers but the power of the cross. Rather than base his proclamation on human reason, common sense, or artful arguments, Paul spoke in halting "fear and trembling" so that if they were to hear and to understand, to assent and to respond, it would have to be solely through "the power of God."

Listening in Order to Speak

"Bishops need to listen," many told me when I was running for the episcopacy. My heart sank. When somebody's talking, I want it to be me. And yet preaching thrives by listening. The twenty-minutes-of-words-worth-saying on Sunday require a preacher who listens all week. Preachers spend years learning to listen to a biblical text honestly, critically, accurately, and humbly—precisely the skills required for leadership listening. We read, go to movies, and download seemingly irrelevant podcasts, all in the hope that the Holy Spirit might pick up something of value for our proclamation of the gospel.

It's always tempting to hunker down with the people who like you and whom you like in return. The skilled pastoral leader creates means for receiving feedback, even (especially) negative feedback. A constant flow of information is required for making good decisions. The great challenge is to uncover information that has been previously suppressed or to hear from people who have not been heard. And then you must decide which feedback is worthwhile. Even as you search for biblical commentaries that are the most helpful in exegeting Scripture, seek out those who can help you honestly exegete, rather than self-protectively *eisegete*, the congregation's situation.

Scripture teaches that when God speaks, it's usually through those who, before God summoned them, were marginalized and voiceless. More important than knowing how to listen is to know to whom to listen. In my first days, eager to show that I was a good bishop, my door was open, so eager was I to listen to anyone, anytime, anyplace. Trouble is, most of the people who wanted to talk, particularly in the first days, came with an agenda: here is work that I want to take off my back and lay on yours. Some of those who were eager to talk to me wanted—even if unconsciously—to warn me not to rock the boat. By manipulating me, they sought to make sure that the power structures that gave them authority over the church were not threatened by a new bishop.

It's axiomatic that most of a good manager's time should be selectively spent with the organization's best people. When the organization is failing, selective listening is even more important and allies in transformation may be more difficult to find because they have been silenced or marginalized by the keepers of the status quo.

A leader must find a way to get the institution talking about issues it has been avoiding for decades. So the challenge is not simply to listen, but also to refocus the conversation by asking the right questions and to give your ear to those who can be most helpful in moving the church forward.

"Good doctors learn to lead with questions and to discipline themselves to delay their answers," said a doctor in one of my congregations. "If I come up with the right diagnostic questions, the patient will tell me what's wrong with them."

Be honest: listening is difficult when you are in a position of authority. By the time you have your ordination credentials in hand and have some church experience behind you, you have probably been trained to talk more than to listen. Congregations crave pastors who give them answers to their problems rather than do the adaptive work of asking questions and encouraging them to help with the answers. Fortunately, the one who leads is also the one who preaches. All good sermons begin with something that has been heard. Biblical exegesis is a series of respectful questions that we ask of a text in the faith that God will give us something to say if we ask prayerfully. Great leaders are questioners and listeners; so are good preachers.

Week-In-Week-Out

I preached a few Sundays ago as a guest preacher. The pastor had asked me for help in his efforts to spur on the dwindling inner-city congregation to undertake the adaptive work of refocusing themselves for the future. I preached as well as I know how, thought I acquitted myself admirably. Maybe I'll even put my sermon on the web.

And yet it was obvious that my words fell on hard ground and didn't take root. My problem was that, in spite of my intentions, I was a visiting prophet who blew in, sounded off, and then blew out. People are well defended against sermons by interlopers like me: too idealistic, doesn't fit our situation, we lack the people and money to do that, you don't understand who we are, that's just not the way we do things around here, and so forth.

While there's something to be said for the guidance of the outside consultant and the visiting expert, there's more to be said for the way in which words spoken by the one who knows and is known are more difficult to dismiss.

The week-in-week-out rhythm of a pastor's sermons, the multiple opportunities enjoyed by pastors whereby they acquire a deep knowledge of a congregation and its strengths and weaknesses—hallway and coffee hour conversations, intimate one-on-one counseling sessions, the sharing and listening on the way to the fall mission trip, the chance supermarket encounters—provide sparks that ignite good Scripture interpretation and relevant preaching.

I left a frustrating Wednesday meeting of the mission committee, depressed by members' lack of energy and commitment. Every good idea (many of them mine) had been shot down. Each attempt to move forward on some mission endeavor was met by a host of objections: we can't, we won't, we shouldn't, not now, not here.

Next morning, I put my pain aside and got to work on my Palm Sunday sermon. It's my usual practice to pray before I begin sermon preparation, something simple, "Lord, give me something to say that you want said. Amen."

That Thursday morning my prayer was heard. I read the assigned gospel:

> As Jesus came to Bethphage and Bethany on the Mount of Olives, he gave two disciples a task. He said, "Go into the village over there. When you enter it, you will find tied up there a colt that no one has ever ridden. Untie it and bring it here. If anyone asks, 'Why are you untying it?' just say, 'Its master needs it.'" (Luke 19:29–31)

This time through this familiar text my eyes fell upon a previously unnoted detail. "Its master needs it." Jesus is preparing for his momentous entry into Jerusalem as the great Passiontide drama begins. At last he shall enter the Holy City and Christ's grand work of redemption shall take place. But none of that can happen without Jesus first enlisting a couple of disciples and giving them a job to do. Rent a donkey. If anyone asks what they're up to, they are to reply simply that the master "needs it."

Can it be that the Messiah, the Holy One of God, the Savior of the World *needs us*? Most of us think of God as the omnipotent, all-sufficient being who needs nothing. Yet Jesus came to us revealing a God who works through delegation, a God who hurts and weeps and thirsts, a God who chooses not to save the world without our help, a God who refuses to work solo. We are the people to whom Jesus gives tasks, those whom he needs. The drama of our salvation is about to begin, and Jesus, in love, needs us, even us.

Though I didn't mention that disappointing committee meeting the week before, when the Palm/Passion Sunday service ended, one of the people, a member of the mission committee no less, grasped my hand and said, "Preacher, got your drift. Let's revisit the idea of a trip to Haiti."

All I did was to fulfill my duty to preach; God did the rest. We preach and lead with confidence that God is determined to have a people in motion.

Repetition

When it comes to articulating the Christian faith, "we can only repeat ourselves," said the great theologian Karl Barth.[1] The theologian does not construct new material but rather repeats the tenets of faith in ways that are heard as fresh and relevant, repeating their historic words in our words, in our time.

One of the weaknesses of my episcopal leadership was that I'm a person who enjoys novel notions, who jumps on new ideas, and who is energized by fresh thoughts. My leadership coach told me, "You are introducing too many proposals. You must focus on what's most important for the church, now, here, and then tirelessly repeat that over and over again."

My conference decided that of all the things we needed, what we most needed were new Methodists. We made growth a conference priority. "Anytime you speak," my coach advised, "before you finish, in some way or another, talk growth."

Sermon series, the three-year cycle of the Revised Common Lectionary, and multiple weekly preaching opportunities give us preachers the ability to repeat ourselves, to keep focused on the Main Thing, to reiterate priorities, and to help the congregation move in one direction.

Ken Blanchard said that a novel idea needs to be communicated at least seven times, seven different ways, before the idea is received by the constituency.[2] Management gurus Chip and Dan Heath tell business leaders, "If you say three things, you don't say anything"[3] (thus demolishing the old "three-points-and-a-poem" sermon model). Relentless, focused communication, continual repetition, and constant clarification are requisites for transformative leadership.

My sixth-grade math teacher could tell you that I've the sort of mind that is prone to wander, is interested in everything, and quickly loses interest in a problem once I've figured it out for myself. I don't like having to go back through my own laborious journey toward a solution in order to invite others to walk the same path. And yet, that is just what interesting preachers do—preach in a way that invites the congregation to repeat the same journey of discovery that led me to the insights in my sermon. A sermon is a venture that begins in the preacher's study and then is recapitulated in the pulpit.

I know a pastor who has led remarkable growth in his suburban congregation. The turnaround began with a congregation-wide assessment and Bible study. The leaders decided that their key vision statement would be Jesus's invitation, "Come, follow me, . . . and I'll show you how to fish for people" (Matt 4:19). Nearly every service, just before the benediction, he asks, "Church, what's our mission?" The congregation responds in unison, "The mission is fishin'."

Cute gimmick or shrewd, memorable repetition? We only repeat what's important, and whatever we repeat becomes important.

Persistence

We preachers tend toward loquaciousness. That's okay because any leader who is guardian of an organization's guiding purposes must be a big talker, relentlessly reiterating the group's core values. The preacher keeps teaching the church to construe the church as a theological, God-produced phenomenon, reiterating our theological identity as the body of Christ in the face of godless explanations for the church. Though the church is a frail, thoroughly human organization, it is not exclusively human, not some sanctified form of Rotary or Kiwanis.

The Trinity is not only the substance of our faith but faith's agent. The Holy Spirit wants to ally with us; we must find ways repeatedly to interject God into the conversation, constantly reminding our people who they are as the people of God, pointing to possible divine incursions into our life together, confident that more is going on in the church than our actions alone.

Chief among pastoral leadership's virtues is repetition's cousin, persistence. Good leaders must be tenacious, persistent, doggedly determined in their service to God and God's people. In Malcolm Gladwell's book *Outliers: The Story of Success*, he puts forth the "10,000-hour rule."[4] What do great musicians, basketball stars, nuclear scientists, football champions have in common? They've all practiced ten thousand hours. Nobody was born that way. No one masters any difficult sport or art without lots of repetitive, persistent practice.

I'll add preaching to Gladwell's "10,000-hour rule." My first ministerial appointment was a two-congregation circuit where I preached four sermons a week. When I complained to an older pastor about the hard work of serving two congregations, he said, "Son, it's a pity it's not three. No better way to learn to preach than having to preach the same sermon four times a Sunday."

Week-in-week-out, in the practice of listening to sermons, Christians are being steadily drawn closer to the heart of God. We are being formed, transformed into the people God has created us to be. If we can be courageous enough to be attentive to a truthful sermon on Sunday, then we may be more courageous in living out the consequences of the sermon on Monday.

Deep institutional change is unimaginable without long-term investment by a leader who lets the congregation know that he or she is in for the long haul.

"It's taken me a year to figure out why you end sermons so abruptly without adequately tying up everything before you finish," a parishioner said to me. "You think that completing a sermon is our job, not yours. You put it all out on the table, help us to see things in new ways, and then it's up to us to tie it together next week."

One year of sermons before they hear? Lord, give me dogged determination.

"What are your disciplines that enable you to persist in the vocation of pastoral ministry?" I hardly ever do a preaching workshop where someone doesn't ask that question. I respond by stressing the importance of regular study, reading and reflection, prayer and meditation. But I have also learned to note the homiletical value of regular interaction with our people in our performance of our pastoral duties.

Whenever my imagination needed stoking, in those times when I've felt depressed and was losing faith in the value of my preaching ministry, I've roused myself and gone forth to visit my people in their homes or places of work. I rarely return from those forays without something to preach. Like John Wesley reluctantly trudging to a meeting on Aldersgate Street, I've even come away from church meetings with an agenda for a future sermon.

Sabbaticals—in which a person unplugs, chills out, and meditates alone in the woods, just me curled up with my books— may be appropriate for the recharging of a professor. Not for a preacher-pastor whose success is judged by what happens in the community and whose work depends upon human connections and interaction. If a pastor fears being on the verge of burnout, an assessment of the value of the work one is doing along with a deeper dive into the life of the congregation are likely to be more rejuvenating than a solitary sabbatical.

Paul's letter to the Ephesians appears in the Revised Common Lectionary in the summer. Why not an Ephesians sermon series? My enthusiasm wilted when my biblical commentary criticized Ephesians as "woefully lacking in larger ethical concerns," preoccupied with rather petty, parochial, intramural, ecclesiastical matters.

This passage is typical:

Don't let the sun set on your anger. Don't provide an opportunity for the devil. . . . Don't let any foul words come out of your mouth. Only say what is helpful when it is needed for building up the community so that it benefits those who hear what you say. . . . Put aside all bitterness, losing your temper, anger, shouting, and slander, along with every other evil. Be kind, compassionate, and forgiving to each other, in the same way God forgave you in Christ. (Eph 4:26–32)

Nice thoughts but modest in scope. That very evening as I dozed through the monthly meeting of the Christian social concerns committee, one of the members, in an argument, made a comment so biting and sarcastic that the person being attacked burst into tears and fled the room. I followed her out into the parking lot. She said to me, "I'll never be on a committee with her again! You shouldn't allow Christians to talk to one another like she talked to me."

I returned to the meeting and groused, "It's ironic that here we sit, discussing how to help people in need outside our church, but can't have a civil conversation with one another in the church."

That night I saw Ephesians 4 with fresh eyes. In my sermon the next Sunday, I told the congregation that Paul wasn't being parochial or petty in urging the church at Ephesus to "[not] let any foul words come out of [one's] mouth." Communitarian Paul says that the toughest but most important work of the church is to be the church, the body of Christ, a showcase to the world of what Jesus can do among ordinary people. Paul says that we are to live our lives, with our fellow Christians, based upon what "is needed for building up the community." How we talk to one another in the church becomes a social justice witness to the world. Just by being "kind, compassionate, and forgiving to each other," we show the world what people look like who live with Christ.

I would have missed that sermon had I not dutifully gone to the meeting.

I spent much of my ministry at a university chapel where my congregation was a floating, ever-changing group of people, most of whom were strangers to one another. My transition from the parish to a university pulpit was a challenge. My wife Patsy said, "You get away with murder in the pulpit because you are such an attentive pastor. How are you going to earn the right to tell the truth when you are not the pastor of most of the people to whom you preach?"

Therefore, I can testify to the ways in which a pastor's daily work—including the pastor's quietly courageous work of leadership—contributes to preaching. At Duke Chapel I had to search for ways to foster some of those theologically rich interactions, difficult conversations, and deep encounters that characterize the lives of most preachers who are pastors. I missed the natural way that a congregation easily moves from proclamation to embodiment.

"Great sermon, but what are we going to do about it?" asked a student after one Sunday service. "I heard way too much 'somebody oughta' in that sermon and too little 'forward march.'"

Sometimes I ended a sermon by saying, "Sharon will be standing at the door with me after service. If God has spoken to you during this sermon, enlisted you for this ministry, Sharon will get your name and we'll get rolling on this right away."

Leadership keeps laying upon our preaching the questions and the dilemmas to which the gospel wants to preach. Preaching keeps renewing our leadership by holding the congregation accountable to the gospel.

Preaching, Managing, and Leading as Complementary

Amanda Olson showed persistent, courageous leadership (combined with competent management) in fostering a conversation on issues of sexuality and gender in her congregation. Note in Amanda's description of the process how her leadership of the congregation fed into her preaching:

> I began small, creating safe space within the church's staff to share perspectives and questions on sexuality, gender, and the Bible. Throughout six months, four team members gathered every other week for 1+ hours to share what we thought and to lovingly challenge each other. We acknowledged our denominational position but allowed for questioning and perspectives outside of that position. We wrestled with key Scriptures and discussed how they fit within the broader biblical narrative and the mission of the church. Initially, it was scary to be vulnerable with such a volatile topic. . . .
>
> Opening up conversation with the church's staff prepared me for the next step in our adaptive process: getting buy-in from the church council. . . . When I first presented the church council with my sense of God's leading me to address human sexuality at Grace, the answer was "not yet." I was disappointed, but the wisdom of the council was good. There were a few reasons that the timing was premature, and I am grateful for their caution. We spent the next few council meetings processing how we [might] address this topic in our local congregation.
>
> Six months later, I launched an adaptive process at Grace by jumping off the high dive. I addressed human sexuality through a sermon series entitled "Sexual Tensions: Seeking Biblically-Faithful Freedom in Christ."

Beginning an adaptive process with a sermon series is not the best approach in all contexts. I know of other congregations who have addressed this topic in adult formation groups or through the organizational structures of the congregation. However, for my context, placing the topic front and center was essential.[5]

Amanda displays a mix of appropriate caution and dogged determination that is the soul of a courageous leader. Preaching was not the whole story of her leadership into this conflicted conversation, but it was essential for "placing the topic front and center."

Note the way that Amanda worked with her church staff and the lay leadership in preparation for "jumping off the high dive" into a sermon series on a topic that would have been too easily dismissed and rejected without her patient, persistent, churchwide preparation. Sometimes our preaching leads a congregation into uncharted waters, the prow of the ship leading into the storm. At other times our sermons are follow-up, helping the congregation reframe and rethink important matters that are being thrashed out in the congregation.

"Got pushback, so I've got to do a few more months' work with my people, in meetings, church school classes, and such, got to have a few more conversations before I take on the topic of mass incarceration from the pulpit," said a pastor who explained his delay in having a conversation with his congregation. "I've got to wait for things to come to a boil, got to wait for the questions to surface. But by God, take it on we will, maybe by Pentecost, maybe after. I'll wait, but I won't let them weasel out of this necessary work, painful though it may be."

Failure in Leadership and in Preaching

Some years ago, in working on a book on clergy burnout, I interviewed dozens of pastors who had called it quits. I discovered that a major reason for leaving the Christian ministry is a pervasive sense, among many clergy, that their work is in vain. They see so few visible results of the effectiveness of their preaching and leadership.

While a graduate student at Emory University, a friend of mine conducted research on the effects of sermons on people's racial attitudes. He skillfully designed a questionnaire to uncover and measure people's racial biases. Then he preached a series of biblical sermons in which he raised the issue of how Christians ought to think about race. Finally, he administered the research questionnaire to them again to see how their attitudes had changed.

In the graduate student lounge he announced the results: his congregation was 2.5 times *more* racist after the sermons!

If you are going to preach or lead with Jesus, you better know how to fail.

The trick, in ministry, is to fail for the right reasons. There is failure that comes from attempting some difficult work and doing it poorly. Spend fifteen minutes in sermon preparation; your sermon is supposed to fail. This sort of flop can be educational.

Then there is the failure that comes from unrealistic or extravagant expectations. A denomination like mine that dares to assign itself a ridiculously unrealistic mission—"Making disciples of Jesus Christ for the transformation of the world"—sets its leaders up for a public dud.

I enjoy reading biographies of great leaders. I'm always impressed with the string of failures that history's best leaders endured along with their success. Many of them would affirm the leadership truism that "I learned more from my failures than from my successes."

Well, good for them. As a kid, I rarely learned as much from an F as from an A. Failure is a great teacher—who sometimes kills the pupils.

After a distinguished church leader had spoken at our Annual Conference, he said to me on the way out the door, "You are doing so many good things to turn around the decline. You are doing just about everything that needs to be done. But sad to say, I think you could be defeated by the demographics. You just can't be an institution where the average age of the membership is sixty years old and expect a dramatic turnaround. Your big challenge is to not allow your determination to be defeated by the numbers."

In a former congregation, when asked by a consultant, "What is your greatest pastoral leadership challenge?" I responded, "Empty Sunday school rooms."

Every day I walked to my study past a half dozen empty Sunday school rooms, one of which had church school literature still on the shelves that questioned the influence of John Kennedy's Catholicism on his presidency! That sort of visible, undeniable failure wears down even the most upbeat pastor.

"Failure is not an option," declared the blustering general in the movie. Such self-delusional braggadocio may be possible in the US Army but not when your mission is assigned to you by Jesus Christ, Son of God, Savior of the World.

As a seminarian, I actually heard H. Richard Niebuhr, after famously defining the church as "the increase of the love of God and neighbor," say, "God help any of you who actually take that goal seriously." The church is, by its nature, a formula for failure.

But what do you expect from people who look at a Jew—who lived briefly, encountered mostly rejection in his ministry, and then died violently in the most humiliating of deaths—and publicly preach, "That's as much of God as we ever hope to see"?

My own teacher of pastoral counseling, James E. Dittes, spoke of "ministry as grief work":

> To be a minister is to know the most searing grief and abandonment, daily and profoundly. To be a minister is to take as partners in solemn covenant those who are sure to renege . . . to commit, unavoidably, energy and passion, self and soul, to a people, to a vision of who they are born to be, to their readiness to share and live into that vision . . . to make that all-out, prodigal commitment to a people who cannot possibly sustain it. . . . The minister is called by their need, by their fundamental inability to be who they are born to be, hence by their fundamental inability to share and live into that vision in which the minister invests all. To be a minister . . . is to be forsaken regularly and utterly, by those on whose partnership one most relies for identity, meaning, and selfhood.[6]

If there's one thing more debilitating to pastoral leaders than failures, it's a timid ministry that attempts so little, that has such a meager vision of the church, that there's never a fiasco. As bishop, I found that one of the most illuminating questions I could ask my pastors was, "What is your most recent failure in your church? What did you learn from it? What might you do differently next time?"

When a pastor replies, "Failure? I can't think of any recent failure," wow, is that revealing. The self-protective meagerness of some pastors' expectations for the church is a sad betrayal of vocation.

It helps, when encountering failure, to be an insatiable learner, the sort of leader who dares to ask, after some undeniable flop, "How did that happen, and how might I do it differently in order to get a different result?"

It also helps to be a preacher. I'm an experienced preacher, and yet, to be honest, I'd say that maybe half of my sermons don't work. The sermon that sounded okay on Sunday begins to smell of failure by late Monday. Preaching is hard work, requiring a mix of intellectual, personal, bodily, social, and spiritual skills. An effective sermon also requires the intervention of the Holy Spirit, God's condescension to use our words as God's word. Preaching is risky business without guarantees. Do your homework, exercise well-honed homiletical skills, and for all your effort, your listeners respond with zombie-like stares and gaping incomprehension.

One of the gifts of being a preacher who is also a leader is learning, at our best, to assemble resources for dealing with the necessary failure that accompanies working with a crucified Savior.

"For three long years I worked patiently but persistently to become that congregation's leader," she told me. "I did what you told me. I brought in a consultant. I attempted to win their trust, to build consensus, to listen to the laity, to get the right people on the bus, just like you taught us in the leadership class. Yet their resistance and intransigence continued. It's then that Jesus told me to shake the dust off my feet and move on. If that church is to be saved from oblivion, Jesus will have to do it through another Presbyterian elder, not me."

As a guest preacher and I vested before the service in Duke Chapel, I said to him, "Peter, I was surprised that you didn't choose to preach from the assigned gospel, going with the epistle instead."

"Oh, I wanted to preach that gospel text; I like nothing better than to beat up on a privileged congregation like yours with a prophetic text like that. But my failures have taught me that I'm not to be trusted with such a text. Brings out the worst in me. My ego gets in the way as I smack them over the head."

Honest self-knowledge—a gift gained by working for a forgiving God—becomes the gospel preacher's greatest leadership asset.

No Guarantees

Sometimes—even though we are preachers who ought to know better—in our leadership failures, we are tempted to grab a surefire quick fix that promises success.

In a field education seminar, students discussed case studies from their summer field work assignments in rural churches in North Carolina. A student presented her case, an account of the irate reaction of a parishioner after her second sermon. It was mostly a short narrative of "I said, and then she said, then I said, then she stormed out."

In the subsequent discussion, questions were asked: Did you think of saying this to her? Are you sure that you delivered your remarks in the right tone of voice? Shouldn't you wait to establish the proper pastoral relationship before preaching tough sermons? Perhaps your inexperience led you to say too much too soon.

We groped for explanations for her preaching failure.

Then one student asked, "Has it occurred to any of us that maybe what the pastor did was right? Here is a parishioner who has learned, through this pastor's ministry, that she did not want to be as close to Jesus as she once thought. Is there a possibility that this is an account of homiletical success rather than failure?"

We had immediately assumed that here we had a problem of improper technique. Surely something was done wrong, an inappropriate word, an improper attitude, a lack of experience, something we could "fix" in this young pastor so that her future sermons would be immune from rejection.

James Dittes contended, quite convincingly, that one reason pastors neglect preaching is that preaching is the pastoral activity that is most frequently prone to failure. In preaching, results are uncertain, negative reaction is always a possibility, and there are few sure indications that our preaching "works."[7]

There are no guarantees because preaching is highly contextual, dependent on a wide array of homiletical gifts, and subject to the machinations of the Holy Spirit. Besides, preaching that is faithful is tethered to the One who lived briefly, failed miserably, died violently, and then rose unexpectedly, returning to the same losers who had betrayed and forsaken him; failure comes with the territory. Some of my homiletical failures are due to my ineptitude; some are due to the difficulties involved in bringing a Savior like Jesus to human speech.

And yet we keep preaching, keep summoning the congregation to greater faithfulness, because the love of Christ compels us (2 Cor 5:14). Despair is not permitted among the servants of a resurrected Lord. The One who was crucified is also the One who, on Easter, was raised. Nothing, not even our ministerial ineptitude, can thwart the final triumph of the reign of God. In the end, God will have God's way with the world, and this world shall be transformed into a new world called "Realm of God." We can confidently face our failures because we believe that we know something that the world does not yet know, namely that this world belongs to the Lamb, and he shall reign. God will have God's say. Without Easter, and the new world that it offers, I cannot imagine how we pastors could have the courage to risk ministry in the name of Jesus. Yet we do because, against all odds, Jesus shall reign.

Even as Jesus returned to the very disciples who had fled from him when the going got rough, greeting them with "As I was saying before I was so rudely interrupted by the cross," so we preachers refuse to let our sin—or that of our listeners—stump us. They can plug up their ears, vote against us, spread nasty rumors about us, or refuse to follow our lead, but they can't thwart a resurrected God's determination to get what God wants.

7

Preaching Is Leading

Though I loved Gil Rendle's *Quietly Courageous*, little about courageous leadership is quiet. Even Gil says that the quietly courageous leader "has the capacity of telling a new story that will get us through the wilderness—the story of hope and promise that does not relieve our anxiety but mobilizes it for a purpose."[1] The major way that Christians are subsumed into and formed by the gospel story? *Preaching.*

In preaching, we lay upon our listeners a better story than any they can come up with on their own. We read them into the pageant of God's salvation of the world, encouraging them to hitch on to what God is doing and to step up and take their bit parts in the drama of redemption.

Rendle says that courageous leaders help the congregation craft a new narrative that tells them where they ought to go. Their new story of themselves may take the form of "Once we were the most prestigious church in this city, but now we are free to be a smaller, more focused and dedicated congregation on the margins of power, yet at the center of God's work in this town." Or "We're going to stop apologizing for having an older congregation and start asking, at every turn in the road, 'What's the unique mission that God has assigned to us in our time and place?'"

The end of any good story is usually unclear at the beginning, which is part of the fun of reading narrative. Why take a journey if you already know the destination? To live out a new story of who we are, we must focus upon proximate purpose rather than our ultimate goal; we must lead without knowing if this is exactly what we ought to do, or if our leadership will land us precisely where we need to be. We must muddle through. Along the way we must cultivate in our preaching and in our leadership a sense of humility, expectancy, and the mystery of God's purposes, determined to stay in conversation, to refuse to walk out when there is anxiety or difficulty, to lead in a timely fashion without working so fast that we don't give folks adequate time to come along with us. We've got to say, "I can't guarantee that this will get us exactly where we need to go, but I am convinced it will head us in the right direction, and I am sure that the way we've *been* going will not get us there."

A good Christian sermon is a biblical sermon, a product of the preacher's priestly listening, in service to the congregation, to the biblical text as it may speak to the congregational context. Leadership is Christian when it submits to the demands that arise out of the story of God's dealings with God's people as narrated by Scripture. Thus Gil says that "a primary task of the quietly courageous leader is to remain aligned with the alternative story of the biblical text."[2] We're accountable, not simply to the wishes of our people or, ultimately, even to the health and vitality of our congregation, but rather to God.

The biblical text holds a privileged place in congregational conversation. As we submit to the biblical text, we are formed and reformed as God's people. We come to accept the text's descriptions of reality as primary and trustworthy. We discover that we live in an ecology in which our actions are not the only action. There will be surprises.

God has convened us, sets our agenda, and holds us accountable. We can't say for sure why God assembled people like us, but we can say wherefore: God's got important work that God refuses to do alone. God enables us, even us, to be faithful. Can we be given the faith to see the present time as a time of open space and surprising possibilities for adventurers in God's grace? In an age of vast biblical illiteracy and widespread confusion about who God is and what God is up to, can we see our age as a divinely given opportunity to preach?

"I was shocked that my new congregation is full of folks who see nothing wrong with the anti-immigration policies of the present administration," said a young pastor. "I don't have to look around for a reason to work hard on my preaching!"

We must truthfully tell a new story about our present reality, deconstructing the old story that has us stuck in one place, being honest about the limitations of that received account of who we are and what we ought to be doing. We must tell the story in such a way that it makes sense to people, offering them new meaning that fits the realities of the present moment in a peculiarly, specifically Christian way. We must help people find themselves in this new story so they get at least a glimpse that this story is theirs.

Sometimes the more skilled the speaker, the more suspicious the constituency. (Some resent President Obama's skilled rhetoric.) There is among many Americans a populist tendency to respond positively to the inarticulate (e.g., Donald Trump). Fortunately, preachers have much experience persuading people through a diverse range of verbal appeals. We have, in our bag of tricks, various ways of overcoming their dismissals when they say, "He's just a smooth talker," or "She's trying to tell me what to do," or "Who are you to say?" Scripture is our model in its dizzying array of literary forms that bring to speech, in spite of our defenses, the truth who is Jesus Christ.

Luke could have presented his Gospel in a straightforward listing of key principles of Jesus. Instead Luke chose to retell some of Jesus's greatest parables that tease, cajole, and entice us toward tough truth. "What is God really like?" the people asked Jesus. He responded, "There was a man who had two sons. His younger son said, 'Dad, drop dead, put the will into effect . . .'" Or, "Who is my neighbor?" Jesus replied, "A man was going down from Jerusalem to Jericho and fell among thieves . . ."

And besides, even when our sermons fall on deaf ears, acceptance of the message by the listeners has never been the supreme test of Christian communication.

Character counts. Presumably, a scoundrel can master church history or theology but not the art of preaching. In my own struggles to be good, I wish it were not so, but it is. There can't be too great a gap between the way the Christian leader tells God's story and the way the leader personally *lives* the story.

Thus the speaker's character is at the top of Aristotle's list of means for rhetorical persuasion. Important character traits of faithful preachers? Submissiveness to the biblical text. Loving Jesus more than we love our congregations. A desire to tell the truth. A willingness to be unpopular. A lifestyle that shows a struggle to be congruent with the gospel. An ability to receive the pain that people often inflict on those who present them with the reality they've been avoiding.

It's disturbing that a recent Gallup poll shows the public's trust in clergy is at an all-time low.[3] Much of this lack of trust in clergy is due not to theological or biblical disagreements between clergy and laity, not to poor preaching, but rather to bad leadership. Catholic bishops who failed to lead accountably have been more detrimental to the lives of millions of believers than any of the bishops' poor sermons. The inability of United Methodist bishops to manage a splintering church has led many Methodists to move from mistrust of their episcopal leaders to disillusionment with our church.

Still, when I see the list of professions the public trusts more than us clergy, I'd like to ask Gallup, "What is the trust we clergy have lost?" Of course laity ought to expect us clergy to be moral exemplars to our congregations. Yet they ought not trust us to be unfailingly compliant and comforting. The church ought to be able to trust its pastor to preach the truth of Christ and courageously lead the congregational embodiment of that truth. In sermons, we preachers must not only narrate a more faithful, truthful story than the one that holds the congregation captive; we also must show that—fellow sinners though we are—we are struggling to embody the gospel and to lead our congregations to do the same. In short, we must be persons who can be trusted to do the task that God has assigned us.

Easter week of 2006, tornadoes cut a swath through Alabama, bringing unimaginable devastation, including the destruction of many churches and parsonages. A week later I stood amid the rubble of a historic church. I had come to comfort them in their grief, but the gospel wouldn't let me stop with only comfort. I was compelled to give them a commission from Christ:

Our gospel comes from the end of the Gospel of John, chapter 21. The end. That's what we thought. "It was a good campaign while it lasted, but we didn't get him elected Messiah. The government turned against us. The crowd voted against him. It's over. Let's go back to fishing, like we were doing before Jesus called us to be disciples. The end."

Right there, at the end, after the curtain has come down on the drama of Jesus, a stranger appears on the beach while they are fishing through the night. From John 21:

> Then the disciple whom Jesus loved said to Peter, "It's the Lord!" When Simon Peter heard it was the Lord, he wrapped his coat around himself (for he was naked) and jumped into the water. The other disciples followed in the boat, dragging the net full of fish, for they weren't far from shore. . . . Jesus said to them, "Bring some of the fish that you've just caught." Simon Peter got up and pulled the net to shore. It was full of large fish. . . . Jesus said to them, "Come and have breakfast." . . . When they finished eating, Jesus asked Simon Peter, "Simon son of John, do you love me more than these?"
>
> Simon replied, "Yes, Lord, you know I love you."
>
> Jesus said to him, "Feed my lambs." Jesus asked a second time, "Simon son of John, do you love me?"

Simon replied, "Yes, Lord, you know I love you."

Jesus said to him, "Take care of my sheep." He asked a third time, "Simon son of John, do you love me?"

Peter was sad that Jesus asked him a third time, "Do you love me?" He replied, "Lord, you know everything; you know I love you."

Jesus said to him, "Feed my sheep." (John 21:7–17)

Simon's story with Jesus wasn't ending; it was beginning, because Jesus showed up and gave him a job to do.

The God of Scripture, the sort of God who came back to us at Easter, has this wonderful way of showing up just as we thought the story was ending, and by showing up, continuing the story, giving the story a more interesting ending than the drama would have had, had there not been a God who loves to raise the dead. Furthermore, he enlists us to play a part in the drama, giving us something good to do in his name. Just as Jesus was the Good Shepherd, he commissions us, even us, to "Feed my sheep."

A large degree of optimism is warranted by the biblical assertion of a God who not only rises from the dead but also brings us back to life by calling us to be his disciples.

A farmer needs workers for his vineyard (Matthew 20). So he arises early, goes out and finds willing workers to harvest his grapes, agreeing with them on the usual daily wage. An invitation has been offered and accepted. End of story.

But as is so often with Jesus, it isn't the end of the story. Mid-morning we are surprised to find the farmer back downtown, hiring more workers for his vineyard, agreeing to pay them "what's right." At noon, mid-afternoon, *one hour before quitting time*, the farmer is out wheeling and dealing, seemingly unable to rest until everyone in town is working in his vineyard. And Jesus says, "God is like that."

Peter, the premier disciple, in the upper room at the end, promises, "Though everyone else desert you, I will not!" Jesus predicts that Peter will fall away before morning. The soldiers appear and drag Jesus away for death. Peter, with the others, scurries into the darkness. Midnight finds him warming himself by a charcoal fire. A little serving girl asks him about Jesus and devastates his resolve. Peter denies Jesus not once but thrice and melts into tears at his failure.

Sometime later Peter and the other disciples have returned to fishing. In the morning, as the sun rises, they see a figure on the beach, cooking over a charcoal fire. He graciously invites Peter to breakfast. It is none other than the Lord who presides over this meal. And then the Lord looks into this betrayer's eyes and commissions him, even him: "Feed my sheep." God is like that.

The dealings between God and us aren't over until God says they're over.

Because of the risen Christ, this church has got to be ultimately optimistic. Prisoners of hope. In spite of our failures as a church and the devastation that sometimes comes our way (like this week we've been through), God keeps recalling us, keeps giving us jobs to do for him. "Feed my sheep."

So I can't stand here today in the ruin of your beloved church building and only weep with you. As a preacher who is answerable to the risen Christ, I've got to tell you: the story between God and this congregation is not over until God says it's over.

Jesus shows up amid our ruin and dares to give us, even us in our grief, a job to do.

Time and again in our journey with Jesus, we think we are standing at Good Friday, only to be surprised that it's Easter. A chapter in your story with God has ended. The building from which you served God for seventy-five years is finished, but God is not finished with you.

With a living, risen Christ, it ain't over until God says it's over. No merely violent, catastrophic tornado can kill a church. It's not over until God says it's over.

I have a feeling that in the coming days some of you will be surprised to discover that your best days as a church are before you; that Christ will not be defeated by death and destruction, much less a terrible tornado; that he shall reign.

And guess who's going to help him?

Witnesses to Resurrection

Preaching and leadership in the name of the risen Christ are not for the faint of heart. It would be one thing to preach about the subject of Christ, but "We preach Christ" crucified and resur-rected (1 Cor 1:21–23). We do not only preach ideas, precepts, and principles; we preach a living, active, resourceful present person, Jesus Christ. Our challenge is well represented by the movements of the risen Christ in John 20. It is "the first day of the week"—that is, the first day of the Jewish work week; the first day when Israel, including the disciples of Jesus, are attempting to get back to normal after a particularly bloody weekend. Their yearning to get back to business will be dis-rupted by the resurrection. Christ will appear among them, kick open their locked doors, and speak to them, command and commission them, and then disappear, moving on, eluding their grasp, refusing serene stability.

That many of us still preach using essentially secular (that is, godless) means of persuasion borrowed uncritically from the world may be testimony to our failure to believe that God raised Jesus Christ from the dead, thus radically changing everything. By relying on communication techniques, we act as if Jesus were still sealed securely in the tomb; as if he did not come back to us, did not speak to us, and cannot—will not—speak today; as if preaching is an exclusively human work that we accomplish through our strategies rather than through the speaking of the risen Christ.

Resurrection is not only the content of gospel preaching but also its miraculous means. Where two or three are gathered in his name, daring to talk about him, he is there, talking to us (Matt 18:20). All the way to the end of the age, in every part of the world, in our baptism and proclamation, he is with us, urg-ing us on (Matt 28:20).

There is that sort of homiletical despair that leads some of our homiletical siblings to quit, to stop talking, and to go into less demanding vocations. Yet there is also that despair, which I find more widespread, that leads some of us to slither into permanent cynicism about the efficacy of preaching.

Their mantra? "Preaching doesn't change people."

Their sense of the pointlessness of preaching may be due to lack of faith that God can do any new thing with us. Accommodate to the sovereignty of sin and death. Yet, how do we know that Easter is not true? Who told us that Jesus used bad judgment when he made us his witnesses to the resurrection even to the ends of the earth?

In order for the powers-that-be to have their way with us, to convince us that the rumor of resurrection is a lie, they must first convince us that death is "reality" and that wisdom comes in the form of uncomplaining adjustment—"This is it. This is all there is. Preaching is woefully archaic, one-sided, authoritarian indoctrination that is bound to fail. Get used to it."

If one considers the evidence for the resurrection of Jesus— the birth of the church from the once despondent and defeated disciples, the perseverance of the saints even unto today, last Sunday's sermon that changed a life, the brief aside in a sermon that took root and bore fruit in someone's soul only months later—it is difficult to see why anyone would disbelieve Easter, except for two reasons:

1. The resurrection is an odd occurrence, outside the range of our usual experience, so that makes Easter a strain upon our conceptual abilities. We tend to reject that which we lack the intellectual apparatus to understand. Because we cannot conceive of resurrection, we deny its possibility.
2. If Jesus is raised from the dead, if the resurrection is true, is a fact, then we must change. Resurrection carries

with it a claim, a demand, that we live in the light of this stunning new reality or else appear oddly out of step. Now we must acknowledge who sits upon the throne, who is in charge, how the story ends. We must either change, join in God's revolution, or else remain mired in the old world and its rulers: sin and death.

Curiously, if there is one thing we preachers fear more than the possibility of crucifixion, it is the potential of resurrection. We have multiple reasons for failure in preaching; success in preaching is an inexplicable wonder that's nothing short of miraculous. Failure in preaching can eventually be accepted, but success in preaching is a summons, an assignment, a kind of scary disruption of our settled definitions of what can and can't be.

If there is one thing we preachers fear more than not being heard, it is being heard, finding ourselves caught up in God's movement into the world, dying and rising, giving birth, rebirth, liberating a life, being a vessel of the Holy Spirit, watching resurrection happen before our very eyes.

Something within me is reassured by declarations that preaching doesn't change people and that my leadership is in vain. I did the best I could. They couldn't step up to the demands of the gospel. They're not really serious about discipleship. Failure is their fault.

Why am I oddly disconcerted when something goes right, when my poor old congregation slips up and acts faithfully, when somebody listens to my sermon and responds, "God spoke to me today. Thanks"? Can it be that my words are not the boundaries of God's word? Is it possible that my leadership of the congregation is not the only pushing, prodding, pleading, and provoking change that is occurring in my church? Might my life as a pastor be more unmanageable and difficult as a result of God's disruptive, life-giving work through my preaching?

Easter can be a greater threat to the stability of my world, to my alibis and excuses, than Good Friday.

Thus because we preachers must, at least on a yearly basis, preach resurrection, we keep being challenged to live and talk as if the women running from the tomb on Easter morning told the truth. We keep being born again into a new reality. And then again. We are not permitted the old excuse for leadership lethargy, "People don't change." Certainly, everything we know about people suggests that they usually don't change. But sometimes they do. And that keeps us preachers nervous, prodding us not to take our cynicism too seriously. Change is rare, virtually impossible, were it not that Jesus has been raised from the dead. When a pastor keeps working with some suffering parishioner even when there is no discernible change in that person's life, when a pastor keeps preaching the truth even with no visible congregational response, when some risky initiative is pushed even though they voted it down twice before, that pastor is being a faithful witness to the resurrection (Luke 1:2). That preacher is continuing to be obedient to the charge of the angel at the tomb to go and tell the news: something has happened that has changed the fate of the world (Matt 28:7). How will the world get the news if no one dares to tell?

Preacher Paul was not only the great missionary to the Gentiles but also living proof that the dead can be raised, thus accounting for his frequent self-referential testimonials of his encounter with Christ. In Paul's encounter, the dead Jesus was not only seen as raised, but Church Enemy Number One, Saul, was raised to new life, given a new name.

Jesus was not just raised from the dead; he *returned* to us; he returned to *us*, to the very ones who had so forsaken and denied him. When he appeared first and most frequently to his own disciples (the ones who, when the soldiers came to arrest him, fled into the darkness), the risen Christ thereby demonstrated that it is of the nature of the true and living God to forgive, and not only to forgive but also to call, commission, and commandeer: "Go! Tell!"

Easter keeps differentiating the church from a respectable, gradually progressive moral-improvement society. In church, there are sudden lurches to the left and to the right, falling backward and lunging forward, people breaking loose and losing control. Easter keeps reminding us pastors that the church is the result of something that God in Jesus Christ has done and is still doing, not something we have done. When the world wants change, the world raises an army, arms itself to the teeth, and marches forth with banners unfurled to storm the ramparts. When the God of cross and resurrection wants to change the world, this God does so nonviolently, through some thin reed of a voice crying in the wilderness—that is, through preachers.

Easter is great grace to those well-disciplined, hard-working, conscientious preachers who are so often in danger of thinking that the kingdom of God depends mostly on their well-constructed and energetically delivered sermons. Easter is also a warning to cautious and too-prudent preachers that they had better learn how to live on the edge. A resurrected Christ is pure movement, elusive, evasive. He goes ahead of us and will not be held by us. A true and living God seems to enjoy shocking and surprising those who think they are tight with God. We therefore ought to press the boundaries of what is possible and what is impossible to say in the pulpit. In our leadership we ought to keep working the edges and exploring organizational possibilities as if miracles were typical of a God who loves to raise the dead. We ought to preach in such a reckless, utterly-dependent-upon-God sort of way that, if God has not vindicated the peculiar way of Jesus by raising him from the dead, then our ministry is in vain. But, as Paul says, thank God, our faith in resurrection is *not* in vain because, by the grace of God, our preaching is not in vain.

Here's a snippet from an Easter sermon that I preached one fall as part of our seasonal stewardship emphasis:

Next week we begin our annual stewardship emphasis. *Stewardship* is a fancy church word for money—what we do with it, what it does with us.

I approach this year's pledge season with trepidation. You, and the risen Christ, made a fool out of me in last fall's stewardship emphasis. Remember? You probably don't recall because the joke was on me, not you.

"You will never make that goal," I pronounced to the finance committee. "We're already 5 percent behind in this year's budget and you are recommending a 10 percent increase! Are you nuts?" I asked them, in love.

"This much of an increase is irresponsible, ill considered, stupid," I told them, authoritatively.

George said, "Preacher, there's a new spirit in this church. We all believe God wants us to be more bold."

I countered, "George, I'm in charge of the spirit here. I'll tell you what God wants and doesn't want. Boldness is not stupidity. Unlike you, I've had theological training."

The finance committee unanimously outvoted me. We launched the October stewardship drive with a 10 percent increase in the proposed budget, and I sat back awaiting my opportunity on a Sunday in November to preach one of my favorite themes: "I told you so."

Mid-October, we paused mid-service for our "Stewardship Moment." Bentley stood up and said, "Never thought I'd make this announcement in this church. You have pledged in full next year's budget!"

Spontaneous applause.

"Which is all the more memorable," Bentley continued, "because our proposed budget increased 10 percent over this year's budget."

Again, applause.

"Now, as I recall, there was someone who said, 'You will never make that budget.' Someone who used words like 'ridiculous' and worse. Help me remember who said that. Somebody said, 'You will never make that budget.'"

"Sit down and be quiet so the service can continue," I said, in love.

Folks, I'm all for resurrection, life over death, the surprising incursions of the Holy Spirit. Yet when God unmasks my own lack of faith, when the enemy of Easter is revealed to be me, well, it makes me look foolish. I've got all these reasons to explain why we can't. Then along comes a resurrected Lord who says, "I'm going to defeat your deadly defeatism. I'm going to show you that this is a better church than you thought it was."

My text is Matthew 28:16–20, the so-called Great Commission:

"Now the eleven disciples went to Galilee, to the mountain where Jesus told them to go. When they saw him, they worshipped him, but some doubted. Jesus came near and spoke to them, 'I've received all authority in heaven and on earth. Therefore, go and make disciples of all nations, baptizing them in the name of the Father and of the Son and of the Holy Spirit, teaching them to obey everything that I've commanded you. Look, I myself will be with you every day until the end of this present age.'"

Jesus doesn't just rise from the dead at Easter; he "comes near" to his disciples and speaks to them. He doesn't just speak to them; he commissions them to go do what he has been doing—make disciples, baptize, and teach all of his commands—promising to be with them every step of the way.

Curiously, in the middle of this dramatic post-Easter moment, this climactic event that's the birth of the church and the launch of the church's mission, Matthew says, "But some doubted."

What did they doubt? Easter? Don't see how they could doubt the truth of the resurrection—there was Jesus standing in front of them, bodily present, clear as day, raised from the dead, speaking to them, giving them directives.

I think what they doubted was not that Jesus was resurrected but that the resurrected Christ, full of authority, raised from the dead and returned to them (even after they had so disappointed him at his crucifixion), *then commissioned them, even them, to go into all the*

*world and do the same work that he had done—making
disciples, baptizing, teaching all of his commands.*

"Who, *us*? Even after all the times we've disappointed you? Us?"

Yes, you. Then Jesus makes one more promise: "Look, I myself will be with you every day." Jesus isn't just raised to life; he is raised to *us*. He commissions disappointingly ordinary people like us to carry on his work, to do his bidding in the world, promising to support, prod, and empower us, even us. The church fathers spoke of Easter as the joke God played on the Devil. We settle in, make peace with the status quo, accept death and defeat as our fate. ("You'll never make the budget.") Then along comes the resurrected Christ, working with us, around us, in spite of us, and it's Easter all over again. ("You have pledged in full next year's budget.")

It's ridiculous—stupid—to think that we, with all of our limitations and inadequacies, are up to being Christ's body in motion in the world—*unless* his promise is true: "I will be with you."

Sometimes, by the grace of God, the leader is led; the one who preaches in the name of Christ is preached to. Sometimes, the joke that God plays on the Devil is an Easter joke played on the preacher.

Thanks be to God!

The Limits of Preaching

As a mix of reason and emotion, preaching can be a valuable opportunity for leadership. In sermons, the pastor can appear to be a confident, trustworthy, courageous, and non-anxious presence in the room. The preacher can direct the congregation toward a purpose more valuable even than caring for the pain within the congregation. The pastor can positively focus upon the strengths, the potential, and the capacity of the congregation more than on their weaknesses and problems.

Preachers help the congregation make sense of their situation. Preaching can defuse the lure of falling back upon what we've always done before or into the temptation of common sense and quick fixes. Preaching enables people to take the long view, to not be defeated by present circumstances, to acknowledge that our actions are not the only actions and that, though we are constrained and limited by our temporality, God is not.

Preachers can notice things and direct attention, reorient a congregation, and suggest a wider array of options, helping to free the congregation from the grip of the status quo. When a congregation doesn't know what to do, they do what they know. Familiar, predictable work keeps them busy clinging to the bank and protects them from having to wade into deeper, threateningly unknown waters.

As a novice I complained to an older pastor about the stubborn conservatism of my congregation. I had preached to them, taught them, and pleaded with them, but still they remained fiercely set in their ways.

"You must disabuse yourself of the idea—stupid, of course, but held by every young preacher—that people will change by simply being told they ought to change, that people will get better because a good sermon demands they get better."

While there is much that the preaching ministry contributes to our ministries of leadership and administration, it's important to admit what preaching can't do:

1. Faithful preaching cannot possibly please everybody. Faithful preaching cannot convince and be comprehended by everybody all the time. Audience reaction to the preaching and parables of Jesus shows that Jesus doesn't mind baffling people then or now.

2. People cannot be talked out of their anxiety and pain; their pain can be acknowledged and respected but not fixed with just the right sermon. Preaching can model and mirror that which the congregation ought to be by verbalizing, articulating, and teaching, but preaching cannot coerce. Preaching can set the tone for congregational discernment and interaction and can model thoughtful deliberation about perplexing issues, but it does not command. A pastor can convey an attitude, a style, a posture that listeners can emulate. The pastor can capture people's attention and can encourage them to focus upon matters they might rather ignore.

3. Not all church issues are best tackled in a sermon. Some important church questions are unaddressed in Scripture; to twist Scripture so it seems to apply to all issues is abuse of Scripture. There are significant crises in the life of the congregation that ought to be resolved through skilled human operative resourcefulness rather than high-flown theological posturing from the pulpit. Other problems are best approached through low-key, give-and-take deliberation, not through one-way pulpit exhortations handed down by the pastor.

The Person of the Preacher

No church is healthier or more focused on mission than its preacher. To preach the gospel without getting in the way of Jesus, to lead without making our leadership all about us, searing self-knowledge is required. Issues related to the personality of the preacher—the preacher's EQ (emotional intelligence), family background, emotional strengths and weaknesses, and lifestyle—have a greater impact upon preaching than does knowledge of sermon construction and delivery. The preacher's capacity for self-knowledge and courageous embrace of his or her own strengths and weaknesses tend to set the upper limits of a congregation's ability to hear their particular truth.

"You didn't preach that sermon just because of Jesus," a parishioner said to me after a humdinger of a sermon on the need for more generous giving in our congregation. She was right. I had allowed my own needs, my resentment, and my fears of congregational financial instability to subsume my duty to preach and to lead.

In a Duke Doctor of Ministry thesis,[4] Jacob Bucholz explored the reasons pastors find it so hard to terminate unproductive church staff. When asked, "Why did you not hold that person to account?" a typical pastoral response is "This job is all that she has. I don't think that the church would stand my being so cruel to her," or other such empathy-based excuses that flatter the pastor's need to appear to be kind and caring.[5]

Jacob concluded that pastors' real reason for inaction is self-protection. We don't want to endure the pain that comes from making tough decisions on behalf of the mission of the congregation. Pastors value preserving the serenity of one-to-one personal relationships more than active, productive engagement with the mission of Jesus Christ.

It's helpful to get as clear as possible about my motives for ministry and the way that my personality affects my preaching and leadership. I've got to find a way to admit to myself which biblical texts bring out the worst in me and which texts I avoid. In what ways does my pastoral humility cover my own adolescent conflicts with authority? How do my theological doubts hinder my proclamation? What conversations cause me anxiety? Which interactions with certain personality types are difficult for me? Some of my critics' comments can be helpful feedback, telling me truth that I'm reluctant to tell myself. My critics may be more emotionally invested in the congregation's future than I: One day I may leave; they're staying. I may serve a half dozen congregations; they know only one.

Some laypeople have expertise in management that I lack. When a layperson says, "Well, you've messed up again and hired the wrong person," you can say, "Can you teach me how to make better staff hires?"

If I'm unable to ask for help or to receive and evaluate criticism, I ought to reflect upon my insecurities or self-doubt that cause me to be defensive.[6]

People are often dishonest with their pastors, so it can be a challenge for the chief truth-teller to be truthful—particularly self-truthful. We preachers are often tempted to see ourselves falsely: "I'm such a prophetic, truthful preacher that nobody wants to follow me because they are all liars and truth-evaders."

Some preachers relish their isolation and regard failure to mobilize the congregation as validation of their superiority.

I think I'm leading for God's sake, but like any disciple who struggles with self-deception, only God knows for sure.[7] My people sin in bedrooms, boardrooms, and classrooms. My sin is worse because the prime location for my sin is the sanctuary. Every time I say to the trustees, "I think Jesus expects us to . . ." or declare from the pulpit, "Thus sayeth the Lord," the possibility for sin is virtually unavoidable. To lead in Jesus's name means to be able to admit to sin, causing me to lead next Sunday's Prayer of Corporate Confession with particular earnestness.

Because both preaching and church leadership are roles bestowed rather than sought, pastors must submit to disciplines that enable us to persevere, even to thrive, in the vocation that God has imposed upon us. What practices aid us in this demanding bifocal calling? The weekly disciplines of sermon preparation—bending our attention to the biblical text, praying that our prejudices will be overcome so that we will be able to hear the text afresh and then have the courage to preach what we have been given—make us better people than we would be if God had not called us to preach. Preaching helps a pastor stay pastoral, driving us back every week to the biblical text from which the purpose of the church and its ministry arise. We climb out of the tug and pull, the muck and mire of the congregation, shake off the praise or blame of our people, mount the pulpit, and dare to say, "The Spirit of the Lord is upon me to preach good news . . ."

Preaching keeps us connected to our originating vocation. One of my fears as a bishop was to wake up one day and be nothing but a sanctified CEO going to meetings, making decisions, shuffling papers. Every pastor ought to pray, "Lord, in order for me to be a more faithful leader, first make me a trustworthy preacher."

Jesus probably preached away more people than he won; the world gave him a cross in response to his preaching rather than a prestigious pulpit. Yet whether we see measurable, positive results or not, we persevere (Heb 12:1) in the faith that Paul knew what he was talking about when he declared that faith comes through hearing (Rom 10:17), and that Jesus had good reasons of his own when he called us to preach and thereby "feed [his] sheep" (John 21:17).

While researching clergy burnout, I became less impressed with the widespread misapprehension that pastoral leadership is so difficult, and the laity are so unfairly demanding, that pastors just burn out.[8] One day they can no longer summon the energy to do the grinding tasks of ministry and, like a rocket running out of fuel, crash and burn.

Burnout is a self-congratulatory metaphor—"I'm so very concerned about the needs of my people, so responsive to their demands, that I just burned out. My Christian over-commitment killed me."

I concluded that something like brownout or blackout better describes why pastors call it quits—it's loss of vision, an insufficiency of meaning and significance rather than a lack of energy. Compelling rationale for ministry seeped away from these pastors, who, having once put their hand to the plow, looked back (Luke 9:62).

It is arrogant for pastors to act as if our bifocal vocations to preach and to lead are so much more demanding than the jobs God gives to the laity. Just this week I received an auto-reply bounce-back from a pastor after I sent her an email: "Thanks for your message. I check email only once a day so that I can focus on my ministry."

The subtheme: "Correspondence with you is a triviality, not real ministry."

The senior pastor of the same church routinely sends out bounce-backs: "Thanks for your email. I'm keeping Sabbath on

Thursdays and do not respond to messages. I will try to return your call within forty-eight hours. If this is an absolute emergency, call the church office." Subthemes: "'Spirituality' means disengagement from my parishioners. I am more spiritual than all of you who can't afford to take a day off."

When I offered to meet with a pastor to discuss his course work, he replied, "No, not on Wednesdays. I save Wednesdays for work on my sermon." Subtheme: "Even though preaching is at the center of Christian ministry, I find it an unbearable burden. Sermons are prepared by detachment from worldly concerns like meeting with you."

At her first meeting with the pastor staff relations committee, the pastor said, "My main concern, as your new pastor, is to protect proper boundaries."

"Boundaries?" one of the laypersons asked.

"Yes," she explained. "In my last church people persisted in calling me after hours, taking time from my family, expecting me to bend my schedule to theirs. I've learned to protect my boundaries for Sabbath and family time."

Protecting personal time was the pastor's *main* concern? It seems not to have occurred to the pastor that she was the only person in the room who was paid to be there.

I have known too many teachers who stay far beyond their classroom hours to work with students in need to buy into the claim that preachers are grossly overworked. No other professionals, certainly not in law or medicine or education, complain as much about their work as do those in ministry—which is ironic since ministry is a vocation, not a profession. If your doctor began your annual physical by saying, "My patients are so cloying, the work of medicine is so impossible, that I must loudly proclaim my craving for leisure," you would go elsewhere for your physical.

Sure, take a day off, spend time in prayer and study, but why make a show of it, implying that God has forced us into an impossible vocation?

I'm unimpressed by the popular belief (fueled by seminary emphasis on "self-care") that pastors are under such crushing stress that we are forced, by our vocation, to be overweight, overstressed, and overworked. Yes, there is stress in ministry, but we owe it to God's calling not to allow that stress to impair our ability to lead the congregation. At times we must free ourselves from the tyranny of our own unrealistic rules, goals, and expectations. The maxims that worked for us in a past church may not represent the leadership and preaching required in a new context.

Sometimes stress is due to factors that have little to do with the difficulties of ministry: we feel stress when we are unqualified or untrained to do the job God has given us to do. An overworked pastor is sometimes an incompetent pastor. The answer to stress in sermon preparation is not a sabbatical sitting in the woods but rather to undertake the hard work of acquiring the homiletical skills we failed to receive in seminary. If we are bound in knots of worry and self-doubt because of our fears related to the church building campaign, we may not need a vacation to Las Vegas as much as we need to swallow our pride and ask for help from those who know more about leadership and management than we do.

"Keeping up a hundred-year-old building with a leaking roof destroyed my marriage."

"My feuding congregation gave me my heart attack."

"I quit because I wanted us to be a more inclusive congregation, but my people wouldn't let me talk about the subject."

These are statements I have heard from pastors. I suspect that all refused to take responsibility for their work, management of their time, and blamed their leadership failures on their people.

Pastors are caregivers, but we must care without allowing the needs of others to subsume our ministry. Pastors are preachers, but we must figure out how to come up with a weekly sermon and still find time, focus, and energy to lead. Pastors are leaders, but we must not allow fear of our followers or love of stability to silence us.

Sometimes we must give it our best shot and then allow someone else to come behind us to complete the work. While giving ourselves fully to our tasks and responsibilities, we must also be able to say, "While this is important work, another will have to lead it."

I've been asked to be the visiting preacher in more than one congregation by a pastor saying, "I'm no good at preaching about money. Will you come and kick off our annual stewardship emphasis?" Me, the hired gun for a pastor who has enough self-knowledge to know he or she is unwilling to put the squeeze on the congregation.

Pastors have been removed for the sin of adultery, and well they should be, but adultery is more easily avoided by a pastor than is vanity. Many parishioners view their pastor with a "halo effect"—my pastor is a very good pastor because she is my pastor. Would I be attending a church with a mediocre pastor?

Surrounded by deferential, flattering sycophants, a pastor is sorely tempted to believe adulators and disregard detractors. Most responses to our sermons, if we get any verbal response, tend to be positive. Though we sometimes complain about the carping criticism of our congregants, most pastors must be intentional in seeking criticism from the congregation.

"I've got four trusted advisors, monitors, and evaluators," the pastor told me, "though none of them know that's their job. At least once a month I check in with them and ask, in effect, 'How am I doing? What's the state of the church?' When I hear criticism from them, I ask, 'Tell me more,' usually followed by, 'Can you suggest someone who could help me do better in addressing this issue?'"

If lying is the mother of vanity, arrogance is vanity's child. Somehow, we've got to get appropriate distance from ourselves and the fulfillment of our needs, distance that's often achieved through ever closer attachment to the Lord who has called us into ministry. A pastor needs "balcony time" (Heifetz) not only from the hassles of the organization but also from the demands of the ego. We pastors must have opportunities to "de-role," to take off the clerical collar and be with friends who are not as preoccupied with the life of the congregation as we, giving us some much-needed distance from the demands of our role and a short vacation from having always to be the spiritual chief.

Preaching is difficult because of Jesus. The sermons he gives us are accountable to a different truth than that lived by nine out of ten Americans. If Jesus had ended his Sermon on the Mount with "Blessed are the lilies," preaching would be easy. Alas, Jesus talked of turning the other cheek, forgiving enemies, and giving to all who ask, thereby making preaching perilous.

While you may lament the low leadership capacity of the average pastor, I remind you that the first and most enduring crisis of leadership was caused by Jesus Christ. Jesus assaulted our definitions of *God* and *Messiah*, and disrupted our notions of leadership. From the first, he predicted that the people in charge would reject him, a forecast quickly validated by his trial, crucifixion, and death.

Right at the beginning, Jesus recruited odd leadership, surprising us by those he called to lead his movement. Yokels whom the world regarded as marginalized, ill-equipped, poorly informed, not particularly spiritual or moral, those of "low account" (1 Cor 1:26–27) Jesus named as disciples, confounding the worldly wise, promising these losers glory in his coming kingdom. In the world, leaders must be omniscient and omnipotent, capable and courageous, competent and creative. Leaders in Jesus's name must simply be obedient to his "Follow me."

> Jesus called [the disciples] over and said, "You know that those who rule the Gentiles show off their authority over them and their high-ranking officials order them around. But that's not the way it will be with you. Whoever wants to be great among you will be your servant. Whoever wants to be first among you will be your slave—just as the Human One didn't come to be served but rather to serve and to give his life to liberate many people." (Matt 20:25–28)

The theological core of the Service of Ordination is the historic *Veni Creator Spiritus*, "Come, Creator Spirit," the epiclesis that the bishop prays for the ordinands. Ministry, which Jesus modeled with basin and towel, is too demanding to do alone. And yet, a prayer for the gift of the Holy Spirit is a dangerous request. The Holy Spirit descends not only with gifts but also with assignments. The Holy Spirit enables intimacy with the Trinity, connecting us not only with the creative Father but also with the suffering of the Son, not only with divine power but also with divinely humble service.

The only good reasons to be in any sort of ministry are theological. Sometimes we do theology while reading books or listening to sermons, and sometimes we theologize by getting our hands dirty, diving into the fray and doing what needs to be done to attend to Christ's body. The only hope we have for accomplishing anything in our church leadership is our faith that Jesus Christ really rose bodily from the dead and that his body is now on the move utilizing the same sort of knuckleheads as those he first called and commissioned.

Ministry, in any of its forms, is always God's idea before it is ours. While we may eventually enjoy our clerical vocation, we do it first of all not because it causes us bliss but rather because it is the job to which God has called us. Jesus loves to summon odd people to painful, impossible tasks. Read the Bible!

All Christian leadership is a gift from God, essential to God's determination to have a people in motion helping God retake what is God's. For those of us called to lead the church, sometimes the great challenge is to believe in the church half as much as God in Christ believes in us, though laity can be forgiven for watching us pastors in action and thinking many things before thinking "gift of God."

Books on leadership tend to say, "Here are the personal qualities you must have, and here are the essential skills you must acquire if you want to lead." Christians are not excused from the self-discipline and the competencies required for effective leadership. However, whereas the authority of the world's leaders is based upon their intelligence, omniscience, proficiency, and creativity, those who have been placed in leadership of the church must simply be obedient to Jesus's "Follow me," confident that God equips those whom God calls, and that God really wants us to succeed in our servant leadership.

Trust me, I'm not the most able of pastoral leaders. Still, in responding to Jesus's vocation, in attempting to conduct my life more in service to the needs of the church than to my personal preferences, in trusting Jesus's faith in me more than my doubts about my abilities, in shamelessly confessing my failures to be the pastoral leader I ought to be, I am given a life more adventuresome than I could have had on my own.

I wonder if that's one reason we preachers, when summoned, answered, "Here am I, send me." Even though we knew little about preaching and church leadership, did we inchoately know that God would transform us into more interesting persons than we would be if left to our own devices? In being forced by God to bend our lives to the leadership needs of the congregation, in standing up and preaching on a tough text even though we received no personal gratification from doing so, in being the unwilling servant who coaxed a congregation to wade into potentially turbulent waters, in having a God more interesting to talk about than us, we are given better lives than we could concoct if God had left us free to worry only about ourselves.

For the good of the church (I hope) and for my great joy (most of the time), I have gotten to play a bit part in the great drama that is God's incarnation in the world, God's loving determination not to work alone, God's relentless resolve to have a family.

Preaching and leading: vocations none of us is good enough to deserve, and gifts of God that give us lives worth living and deaths worth dying. Thanks be to God!

NOTES

Chapter 1

1. Eugene H. Peterson, *Subversive Spirituality* (Grand Rapids: Eerdmans, 1997), 30.
2. Christopher A. Beeley, *Leading God's People: Wisdom from the Early Church for Today* (Grand Rapids: Eerdmans, 2012), 14.
3. P. T. Forsyth, *Positive Preaching and the Modern Mind* (London: Independent Press, 1907), 53–68.

Chapter 2

1. From William H. Willimon, *Accidental Preacher: A Memoir* (Grand Rapids: Eerdmans, 2019), 194–95.
2. Herman Melville, *Moby Dick* (New York: Bantam, 1981), 46.
3. See a larger portion of Turner's sermon in William H. Willimon, *Who Lynched Willie Earle? Preaching to Confront Racism* (Nashville: Abingdon, 2017), 87–88.
4. Martin Luther, "The Sermon on the Mount," in *Luther's Works*, vol. 21, ed. J. Pelikan and H. T. Lehmann (St. Louis: Concordia, 1967), 9.
5. Luther, "Sermon on the Mount," 9.
6. William H. Willimon, sermon preached September 20, 2005, in Louisiana.
7. William H. Willimon, sermon preached September 1982, Northside United Methodist Church, Greenville, South Carolina.

8. Edwin Friedman, *A Failure of Nerve: Leadership in the Age of the Quick Fix* (New York: Seabury Books, 2007), ix.

9. See my account of what I learned as a bishop in William H. Willimon, *Bishop: The Art of Questioning Authority by an Authority in Question* (Nashville: Abingdon, 2012).

10. Christopher A. Beeley, *Leading God's People: Wisdom from the Early Church for Today* (Grand Rapids: Eerdmans, 2012), 8.

11. Friedman, *Failure of Nerve*, 126.

12. William H Willimon, *Growing Old in the Church* (Grand Rapids: Brazos, 2019), 29.

Chapter 3

1. Peter F. Drucker, *Managing the Nonprofit Organization: Principles and Practices*, reprint (New York: HarperCollins, 2005), 151.

2. Quoted by John H. Leith in *John Calvin and the Church: A Prism of Reform*, ed. Timothy George (Louisville: Westminster/John Knox, 1990), 212.

3. Walter Brueggemann, in *The Church as Counterculture*, ed. Michael L. Budde and Robert W. Brimlow (Albany: State University of New York, 2000), 53.

4. William H. Willimon, *Proclamation and Theology* (Nashville: Abingdon, 2005), 20.

5. *Calvin: Institutes of the Christian Religion,* ed. J. T. McNeill, trans. F. L. Battles, Library of Christian Classics (Philadelphia: Westminster, 1960), 4.24.12

6. Ronald A. Heifetz, *Leadership without Easy Answers* (Cambridge, MA: Harvard University Press, 1994), 74.

7. I give a full account of Hawley Lynn's sermon and its significance in America's racial history in William H. Willimon, *Who Lynched Willie Earle? Preaching to Confront Racism* (Nashville: Abingdon, 2017), 148.

8. Heifetz, *Leadership without Easy Answers*, 128. Timing is also discussed in Ronald A. Heifetz and Marty Linsky, *Practice of Adaptive Leadership: Tools and Tactics for Changing Your Organization and the*

World (Cambridge, MA: Harvard Business Review Press, 2009), 44–45.

9. Eugene Lowry, *The Homiletical Plot: The Sermon as Narrative Art Form* (Louisville: Westminster John Knox, 2000).

10. Gil Rendle, *Quietly Courageous: Leading the Church in a Changing World* (New York: Rowman & Littlefield, 2019), 71. My thoughts on church leadership are heavily indebted to Rendle's book.

11. John P. Kotter, *Leading Change* (Cambridge, MA: Harvard Business School Press, 1996).

12. The best book on church management is John W. Wimberly Jr., *The Business of the Church: The Uncomfortable Truth That Faithful Ministry Requires Effective Management* (New York: Rowman & Littlefield, 2010).

13. Adapted from Anthony B. Robinson, "Leadership That Matters," *Christian Century* 116 (December 15, 1999): 1228–31.

Chapter 4

1. William H. Willimon, ed., *Sermons from Duke Chapel: Voices from "A Great Towering Church"* (Durham, NC: Duke University Press, 2005).

2. Gil Rendle, *Quietly Courageous: Leading the Church in a Changing World* (New York: Rowman & Littlefield, 2019), 34. Gil takes this dichotomy of convergent and divergent from Charles Handy of the London School of Business.

3. William H. Willimon, *Worship as Pastoral Care* (Nashville: Abingdon, 1982), 198–99.

4. Peter L. Steinke, *How Your Church Family Works: Understanding Congregations as Emotional Systems* (Herndon, VA: The Alban Institute, 2006), 130.

5. Martin Luther King Jr., "Letter from a Birmingham Jail," in *Letters to a Birmingham Jail: A Response to the Words and Dreams of Dr. Martin Luther King, Jr.*, ed. Bryan Loritts (Chicago: Moody, 2014), 22.

6. King, "Letter," 22.

7. King, "Letter," 22.

8. See the account of the lives of the recipients of King's letter in Jonathan Bass, *Blessed Are the Peacemakers: Martin Luther King Jr., Eight White Religious Leaders, and the "Letter from Birmingham Jail"* (Baton Rouge: Louisiana State University Press, 2001).

9. Thomas G. Bandy, *Mission Mover: Beyond Education for Church Leadership* (Nashville: Abingdon, 2004), 68–70.

10. Paul D. Borden, *Hit the Bullseye: How Denominations Can Aim the Congregation at the Mission Field* (Nashville: Abingdon, 2003), 28–30. Borden works similar themes in *Assaulting the Gates: Aiming All God's People at the Mission Field* (Nashville: Abingdon, 2009).

11. Karl Barth, *The Göttingen Dogmatics: Instruction in the Christian Religion*, trans. Geoffrey W. Bromiley (Grand Rapids: Eerdmans, 1990), 45–51.

12. Rendle, *Quietly Courageous*, 103.

13. Ronald A. Heifetz and Marty Linsky, *The Practice of Adaptive Leadership: Tools and Tactics for Changing Your Organization and the World* (Cambridge, MA: Harvard Business Review Press, 2009), 44.

14. Ronald A. Heifetz, *Leadership without Easy Answers* (Cambridge, MA: Harvard University Press, 1994), 68.

15. Jim Collins, *Good to Great: Why Some Companies Make the Leap . . . and Others Don't* (New York: HarperCollins, 2001).

16. Rendle, *Quietly Courageous*, 128.

17. Peter L. Steinke, *How Your Church Family Works*, 124.

18. Rendle, *Quietly Courageous*, 131–32.

19. Abby Kocher, "David and Goliath: 1 Samuel 17:32–49" (sermon, Salem UMC, Morganton, NC, June 28, 2015), in William H. Willimon, *Who Lynched Willie Earle? Preaching to Confront Racism* (Nashville: Abingdon, 2017), 128.

Chapter 5

1. WA 25:253, as quoted by Charles Campbell, "Resisting the Powers," in *Purposes of Preaching*, ed. Jana Childers (St. Louis: Chalice, 2004), 25.

2. Ronald A. Heifetz, *Leadership without Easy Answers* (Cambridge, MA: Harvard University Press), 156, 265.

3. Lovett Weems Jr., *Take the Next Step: Leading Lasting Change in the Church* (Nashville: Abingdon, 2003), 114–15.

Chapter 6

1. See William H. Willimon, *Conversations with Barth on Preaching* (Nashville: Abingdon, 2010), ch. 3.

2. Ken Blanchard and John Britt, *Who Killed Change?* (New York: William Morrow, 2009), 132.

3. Chip Heath and Dan Heath, *Made to Stick: Why Some Ideas Survive and Others Die* (New York: Random House, 2007), 33–34.

4. Malcolm Gladwell, *Outliers: The Story of Success* (New York: Little, Brown, 2008), 39–42.

5. Amanda L. Olson, "Out of the Church Closet: Hope for the Evangelical Covenant Church and Sexual Minorities in the Local Congregation and Beyond," Doctor of Ministry Thesis, Duke University, 2019.

6. James E. Dittes and Donald Capps, eds. *Re-Calling Ministry* (St. Louis: Chalice, 1999), 15.

7. Dittes and Capps, *Re-Calling Ministry*, 123–37.

Chapter 7

1. Gil Rendle, *Quietly Courageous: Leading the Church in a Changing World* (New York: Rowman & Littlefield, 2019), 219.

2. Rendle, *Quietly Courageous*, 86.

3. Griffin Paul Jackson, "The 7 People Christians Trust More Than Their Pastors," *Christianity Today*, January 4, 2019, https://tinyurl.com/yxzgh369.

4. Jacob Bucholz, "Managing Church Staff with Authority: A New Model of Servant Leadership," Doctor of Ministry Thesis, Duke University, 2019.

5. Rendle, *Quietly Courageous*, 173–92, does a fine analysis of empathy as an excuse for poor leadership.
6. See Douglas Stone and Sheila Heen, *Thanks for Your Feedback: The Science and Art of Receiving Feedback Well* (New York: Penguin, 2014).
7. See Arbinger Institute, *Leadership and Self-Deception: Getting Out of the Box* (Oakland, CA: Berrett-Koehler, 2014).
8. William H. Willimon, *Clergy and Laity Burnout* (Nashville: Abingdon, 1989).

INDEX OF NAMES

INDEX OF NAMES

SCRIPTURE INDEX

Compelling and timely books on biblical preaching.
Good preaching changes lives!

Working Preacher Books is a partnership between Luther
Seminary, WorkingPreacher.org, and Fortress Press.

Books in the series include:
Preaching from the Old Testament by Walter Brueggemann

Leading with the Sermon: Preaching as Leadership by
William H. Willimon